LIFT YOUR SPIRITS

THE SOUTHERN TABLE

Cynthia LeJeune Nobles, Series Editor

LIFT YOUR SPIRITS

A CELEBRATORY HISTORY OF COCKTAIL CULTURE IN
NEW ORLEANS

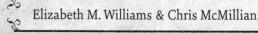

Elizabeth M. Williams & Chris McMillian

FOREWORD BY DALE DEGROFF

Louisiana State University Press

Baton Rouge

Published by Louisiana State University Press
Copyright © 2016 by Louisiana State University Press
All rights reserved
Manufactured in the United States of America

FIRST PRINTING

DESIGNER: Barbara Neely Bourgoyne
TYPEFACE: Sina Nova
PRINTER AND BINDER: Maple Press

LIBRARY OF CONGRESS CATALOGING-IN-PUBLICATION DATA

Names: Williams, Elizabeth M. (Elizabeth Marie), 1950– author. | McMillian, Chris, 1961– author.
Title: Lift your spirits : a celebratory history of cocktail culture in New Orleans / Elizabeth M. Williams and Chris McMillian ; foreword by Dale DeGroff.
Description: Baton Rouge : Louisiana State University Press, [2016] | Series: The Southern table | Includes bibliographical references and index.
Identifiers: LCCN 2015042803 | ISBN 978-0-8071-6326-9 (cloth : alk. paper) | ISBN 978-0-8071-6327-6 (pdf) | ISBN 978-0-8071-6328-3 (epub) | ISBN 978-0-8071-6329-0 (mobi)
Subjects: LCSH: Drinking of alcoholic beverages—Louisiana—New Orleans— History. | Cocktails—Louisiana—New Orleans—History. | Prohibition—Louisiana— New Orleans—History.
Classification: LCC GT2883.U6 W55 2016 | DDC 394.1/30976335—dc23
LC record available at http://lccn.loc.gov/2015042803

To my parents, Cleve and Jo,
for teaching me to drink

—E.W.

To my wife, Laura, and our children

—C.M.

CONTENTS

ILLUSTRATIONS

FOREWORD

> No matter where it went, the Museum of the American Cocktail stayed
> connected to New Orleans. Why New Orleans? . . . MOTAC belonged in
> New Orleans because New Orleans was the place that nurtured the
> cocktail. The city was the keeper of the cocktail flame.
>
> —from this book's last chapter

We opened the Museum of the American Cocktail in New Orleans in 2005, and that first year we began marking certain days as important in the calendar of cocktail culture: May 13, 1806, the day that *cocktail* was first defined in print; and December 5, 1933, the day Prohibition was repealed. We celebrated those days at the museum, and we encouraged bars and bartenders around the country to join us in that celebration.

Among the founders of the museum were Chris McMillian and his wife, Laura. Chris was already a scholar of the New Orleans drinks culture and the celebrated barman at the Library Lounge in the Ritz-Carlton. Chris adopted New Orleans as home for himself and his family in 1984, but it was a homecoming. Chris was made for New Orleans, and he has enriched and added to the drinks culture; he is timeless but timely, a storyteller and an oral historian. In *Lift Your Spirits,* we are his and Elizabeth Williams's captive but willing audience.

By Repeal Day 1933, the fine craft of cocktail bartending as a profession had all but disappeared, and criminal organizations had a firm grasp on the sale of alcoholic beverages. In 1932, Franklin D. Roosevelt rode to the White House on the repeal ticket, but to actually amend the Constitution required a series of delicate maneuvers that Roosevelt and a group of industry leaders skillfully executed to reverse the Nineteenth Amendment.

The compromises Roosevelt made specifically with states' rights advocates turned over the control and sale of alcoholic beverages to the states and even local counties, resulting in a byzantine maze of "blue laws" that confounded legitimate purveyors of spirits from state to state—but not in New Orleans. In New Orleans, the drinks culture was integrated tightly into the fabric of daily life, and Prohibition was greeted with an almost comical shrug.

Throughout the United States, except in New Orleans, the rich culture of drink that had developed over more than two centuries unraveled during the 13-year-long social experiment. After Prohibition ended, desperate economic times and another world war stalled the revival of the fine spirits industry. Many fine spirits brands that contributed to a rich palette of flavors did not survive the decade-plus drought.

The bottom of the barrel was hit during peacetime in the fifties, when the drinks industry suffered the ultimate insult, shortcuts to make up for a lack of skilled labor. There was no serious training available for this "gangster" trade, so bar and restaurant owners turned to presweetened, artificially flavored mixes in an attempt to offer a consistent product. They succeeded; they achieved a consistently mediocre product—even in some bars in New Orleans—but not in all.

On the culinary side of the business, pre-prepared, canned, and pro-cessed food products developed during the world wars were embraced by the commercial food industry. Designed to make life easier, these products flooded the market; TV dinners, baby formula, Kool-Aid, Jiffy Pop, and Tang were the rage. Americans all over the country happily abandoned the fresh and natural, scooping up all that was processed and canned—but not so much in New Orleans.

New Orleanians were never in danger of losing their culture of food and drink. It is the foundation of their way of life. In *Lift Your Spirits*, Williams and McMillian reveal a city that absorbed without destroying cultures: Spanish, French, and American. The cuisines that are celebrated in the diners and pubs, neighborhood groceries, and signature restaurant destinations are the first fusion cuisines in America. The iconic dishes with tradition never disappeared, and the drinks that have defined New Orleans for over 120 years are still the cornerstone of the drink culture.

My first experience of New Orleans occurred in 1978. My girlfriend and I were on a road trip from New York to California when we wan-dered into the Old Absinthe House just as the bigger-than-life character behind the bar was shouting "SAZZERRRAAAC" and tossing a glass in the air. We felt a fine mist on our faces and smelled a slight aroma of anise or licorice or both. When we finally fell under her gaze, we ordered Sazeracs. There were thousands and thousands of business cards stapled to the wall, and at the corners of the bar, tall stone and brass fountains sat unused, relics of an earlier time. We were strangers in a strange land and stayed two days beyond our planned stopover.

In the years to come, I ordered Sazeracs at Tujague's on Decatur, Jacques-Imo's uptown, the Carousel Bar at the Monteleone. I ordered them with one lump instead of two—I like them on the dry side—and in each of these places I found surroundings of substance. They were worlds unto themselves with their regulars and streams of guests from around the globe, all drawn to New Orleans by the promise of hospitality and of a bit of the naughtiness that New Orleans culture celebrates.

In 2003 I jumped at the chance to become a part of Tales of the Cocktail, a Brown-Forman–sponsored celebration of New Orleans cocktail bars hosted by Ann Rogers, now Ann Tuennerman. Ann convinced a group of beverage professionals from around the country to participate in a two-day event celebrating the New Orleans drinks culture and the hometown brand Southern Comfort. Thirteen years later, Ann has shared her home with thousands from around the world who have added touches of their culture and changed her city once more. They have made the fabric just a bit richer; the colors a bit deeper.

I made the pilgrimage to 437 Royal Street to stand in the shop where Antoine Amédée Peychaud operated his apothecary and formulated the bitters recipe still used to make Sazeracs. Today, Steve Cohen and his son Barry own the shop, selling old coins, vintage firearms, and artifacts from sunken Spanish galleons.

Steve came out of the back room with a large antique bottle of dark-colored glass with the words "Peychaud's Bitters" and a Magazine Street address legible on the side. That's farther uptown from our location on Royal Street. "Peychaud had two shops," Steve explained. "I wish I could find the bottle with our Royal Street address on it." He was proud of the heritage and history of his store. Steve's great-granddaddy had purchased the shop in the late nineteenth century, sold all the old apothecary bottles, and begun the antique and curio business.

New Orleans is home to a special tribe who love their history and culture but who live the present with passion, embrace their diversity, and take enormous pleasure in sharing it all with strangers who wander into this foreign land that doesn't remotely resemble the places where they live.

Elizabeth Williams and Chris McMillian have opened a window to an amazing past, and they also welcome us to join them in the city they live in today, the city they love. The rest of the country is nice to visit, but they couldn't live there.

—Dale DeGroff
Founder, Museum of the American Cocktail
October 2015

LIFT YOUR SPIRITS

INTRODUCTION
THE CITY, THE CULTURE, AND THE COCKTAIL

Times are not good here. The city is crumbling into ashes. It has been
buried under a lava-flood of taxes and frauds and maladministrations so
that it has become only a study for archaeologists.... But it is better to live
here in sackcloth and ashes than to own the whole State of Ohio.

—LAFCADIO HEARN, 1880

New Orleans has been fueled by cunning, imagination, and liquor
since its founding. In addition, the city has always had a reputation
for tolerance, for self-reflection (some say self-absorption), and
for a reluctance to change. New Orleanians care deeply about tradition
and about being connected to the past. And they respect the need to
celebrate, to console themselves, and to carry on, almost always accompanied by alcohol.

The cocktail wasn't invented in the Crescent City—an early definition
is found in a New York broadsheet of 1806—but historical accuracy
doesn't stop many New Orleanians from asserting that claim. The city's
history and culture make it both plausible and believable. Where else
could the cocktail have been created, if not in New Orleans? And since
New Orleans was influenced by the drinking habits of wine- and spirit-
loving French and Spanish settlers, this story has deep roots.

Chris McMillian is part of a long line of bartenders in New Orleans—including Joseph Santini and Henry "Carl" Ramos—who have respect for the craft, for the customer, and for the culture. In these pages, we will explore just what it is about New Orleans that has made it the defender of the cocktail and a tolerant haven for drinkers. While many people today come to New Orleans from other, more sober places in order to get drunk, those of us who live here know that getting drunk is for amateurs. We drink for pleasure and because alcohol is a social lubricant, enhancing the experience of many occasions. We drink because cocktails and spirits taste good. We drink as a way to share time together with friends and strangers alike, which is why so many cultural events include alcohol. The novice visitor sees easy access to alcohol but lacks training in moderation and the cultural overlay, and thus often fails to grasp the whole picture. He or she can misinterpret tolerance of drinking and a *joie de vivre* with simple license to drink to excess. And doing so ignores the unique history of the city's drinking culture.

The United States' purchase of the Louisiana colony in 1803 ushered in the American period of New Orleans. While that era continued to shape and nurture the importance of drinking in the city, the drinking culture rested on a French and Spanish colonial legacy. That continental European history created an environment that was different from the rest of early America, allowing New Orleans to remain a place apart. Thanks to its thriving port, this city developed into a metropolis teeming with goods and people from all over the world. And visitors drank, communed, and experienced the welcoming embrace of its watering holes. They brought their drinking expectations and experiences with them, leaving their own marks on the places in which they drank, as well as taking a little piece of New Orleans away with them to wherever they were going.

Even today, public drinking in the city is observable on a regular basis. The city's open container law is extremely liberal. Drinking can accompany a picnic in the park. Those fishing at the edge of Lake Pontchartrain can enjoy alcoholic refreshments while contemplating a bobbing cork. People of drinking age can drink outside on the street, although there is a nod to public safety in the requirement that alcoholic beverages not be consumed from a glass container. At public celebrations such as Mardi Gras, St. Patrick's Day, and St. Joseph's Day parades, or Halloween, drinking can be observed at night and during the day. And yes, there are still drive-through daiquiri shops dispensing frozen alcoholic treats, although today they are sold in covered containers. Too, New Orleanians are no longer allowed to drive with a beer in hand, but single cans of beer are sold at gas stations all over the city.

It is a common story repeated by many that when New Orleanians first leave the city, they discover that the rest of the country does not understand the go-cup. In New Orleans, when you are ready to leave a bar or a restaurant and have a bit of drink left in your glass, you do not have to gulp it down; you can ask for a plastic cup to take leftovers. It is a common cultural practice. Just as you can take your extra food home in a doggie bag, you can continue drinking your drink in a go-cup. And just as you can get your food to go, at some places it is possible to purchase your drink to go.

When you ask for a go-cup in another city or state, the bartender or wait staff is likely to stare at you with incomprehension. The savvy bartender might ask if you are from New Orleans before explaining that there are no go-cups allowed. Many bars and restaurants in New Orleans have specially branded plastic cups, so that patrons advertise that particular bar or restaurant as they walk down the street. Many of those plastic cups wind up in your cupboard, reminding you later of that bar or restaurant. The specialty plastic cup was invented in New Orleans by Corrado Giacona at Giacona Container Corporation. They give great publicity, and are also thrown, branded with a Mardi Gras krewe's name and date, during parades throughout the Carnival season.

With all the tourists who flock to New Orleans looking for a quick drunk, a pessimist can rail against the disintegration of the city's cocktail culture, blaming it on the rise of a certain kind of tourism. Many tourist bars use bottled juices instead of fresh, and powdered or bottled mixes to which one just adds liquor. Large, overly sweetened drinks that mask the kick of the alcohol and leave imbibers thirsty became all the rage after World War II, and they can still be found in many places. But with the resurgence of the craft cocktail across the United States and around the world, New Orleanians are enjoying the traditional cocktails that they have always incorporated into their cultural celebrations.

Over the past decade, cocktail events such as the Tales of the Cocktail festival have enjoyed tremendous success in the city. But even after being exposed to the latest in craft cocktail trends, during the event's first few years New Orleanians clung to their old ways of convenience over quality. The rise of the craft cocktail movement in the city was actually kickstarted by nonlocal craft cocktail bartenders who came to New Orleans to celebrate the cocktail. That movement was developing in other cities, but it had not really reached New Orleans when visitors came to the first few years of Tales; individual craft bartenders flourished, but the audience was not yet developed. Now, however, New Orleanians are embracing the new craft cocktails so many local bartenders are introducing, and which are often made with house-made bitters and liqueurs. And in sync with the traditional nature of the city, many craft bartenders are preserving and cherishing the proper making of the original, now traditional, cocktails.

Today, the city provides three basic levels of cocktail experience. Tourist bars serve enormous sweet drinks—often with colorful names and signature glasses—that pack a great deal of wallop. The allure of these bars and drinks is irresistible to tourists who have a superficial understanding of the city as a party town, especially those looking for an inexpensive, naughty walk down Bourbon Street. On many neighborhood street corners, dive bars welcome regulars and provide a traditional meeting place for swapping stories and keeping up with local gossip. The bartenders at these bars may serve a standard cocktail made with bottled juices and mixes. The customer knows what to expect and gets it. And finally, craft cocktail bars flourish as places where bartenders approach mixing drinks as a chef approaches the preparation of a meal, preparing bitters and liqueurs in house and using fresh ingredients. Often these bartenders are well-known personalities, performing their magic behind the proscenium that is the bar.

The craft cocktail is also making its way into home bars. No longer are people using packaged mixes and bottled juices to the exclusion of fresh ingredients. Local liquor stores proudly display a range of bar equipment for sale to the home bartender. The resurgence of the craft cocktail is merely one more phase in the evolving history of the cocktail in New Orleans. And bringing this crafted experience into the home means that it will be incorporated into the cocktails that are traditional parts of private celebrations and cultural events.

Even though the city is moving forward, a note about Hurricane Katrina and its impact on the city's psyche is in order. As refugees scattered around the country in the aftermath of the Katrina floods, they wondered when and whether New Orleans could become home again. After all, members of Congress were talking about not rebuilding the city. But seeing how people lived in other parts of the country made New Orleanians understand how precious the rhythms and culture of their everyday life really were, and they missed everything, from their music to red beans and rice to their cocktails. And not only the cocktails themselves, but the way people drank in general.

Many people learned about state liquor laws the hard way, when they found out that they couldn't pick up a bottle of bourbon at a local drugstore, or that they couldn't have a beer at a picnic in the public park. Theirs was not only a wrenching experience of despair at having lost everything and being uprooted for an indefinite period. Theirs was also the experience of the need to live a certain way, as a part of their identity, and being denied the ability to be themselves.

Those who did not evacuate and who lived in the 20 percent of the city that did not flood, which included the French Quarter (known locally as the sliver by the river), were able to celebrate publicly with each other with drinks. People shared their stashes of alcohol, albeit often drinking it warm. Merchants readily acknowledge that right before a hurricane, when people are buying batteries and water, they also stock up on alcohol for hurricane parties. In the face of a hurricane or in the time after a hurricane while waiting for power to return, drinking is a common local method of coping.

When New Orleans was drained of the water that stood in the city for three weeks, when electricity was restored, and when water was once again potable, residents began to return. And they came back with a resolve to confirm the city's identity. Some publicly worried that New Orleans would turn into a boutique city, a Disneyland version of what it had been. But they forgot that New Orleans has experienced fires and floods throughout its history. Every time, the city simply takes up life again. And every time it becomes more iconically New Orleans.

That is just what happened after New Orleans reopened. As people returned, they sought out restaurants and bars that were serving old favorites. Sazeracs were drunk together in solidarity, even by people who might not normally order them. People told stories of not being able to purchase various sought-after and culturally necessary products, such as filé or Peychaud's bitters, finding others who had experienced the same deprivation. While in exile, they had also experienced the same lack of understanding of why what they wanted was important, even from sympathetic supporters outside of the city. Back and together with other New Orleanians, people recommitted to the city by engaging once again in its traditions. In support of one of its customs, they drank good cocktails, together.

While once on the cutting edge of modernity, today's New Orleans is the keeper of the flame of tradition. We preserve our buildings, our cuisine, our music, and our culture. We sell the opportunity to observe tradition, too, to tourists who come to experience it. We do not reject modernity; we simply do not seek to be in the forefront of change. We observe as society evolves and join the train in the end after we have worked out how to preserve our culture and be modern as well. All that said, this book is simply the exploration of the history, the culture, and the soul of New Orleans as reflected in the cocktail. To help you shake together some of the cocktails enjoyed in New Orleans, we're including iconic and innovative recipes from local bars and mixologists, as well as from the authors. Please read and enjoy, drink in hand.

COLONIAL
NEW ORLEANS

She [the Native American] began to smile, and said many things
which I did not comprehend, but she made me understand by signs,
that there was no occasion for a gun to kill such a beast.

—ANTOINE LE PAGE DU PRATZ

upon seeing an alligator, from *The History of Louisiana* (1774)

New Orleans has always been a city apart. While much of America was colonized by men and women seeking religious freedom and establishing themselves in New England and along the Atlantic coast, New Orleans—surrounded by water and close to the Gulf of Mexico —invented itself with a different point of view. Founded as a French colony in 1718, New Orleans was intended to be a source of profit for the French crown. The fledgling city quickly became a destination not only for colonists, but also for people who were deemed undesirable in France. Many petty criminals, vagrants, and debtors were treated to a one-way trip to la Nouvelle-Orléans. Perhaps because of the rough-and-tumble beginnings of the city, its Roman Catholic inhabitants developed a great tolerance for individualism and idiosyncrasies. In stark contrast to the earnest and righteous roots of the Protestant United States, New Orleans has always been a place with its tongue poked permanently against its cheek and its arms wide open in welcome.

✣ WINES ✣

Although coffee became a popular beverage in the eighteenth century, New Orleanians drank copious amounts of wine as well, whether in coffeehouses, at taverns for travelers, or in the home with meals. Just as shared food was considered an essential form of hospitality, the sharing of wine (or other spirits) was seen as a gesture of welcome. Wine also was an important part of Roman Catholic religious ritual, and as a French colony, New Orleans was a Catholic town. For many reasons, therefore, it was important to ensure an adequate supply of wine. But doing so proved to be a challenge.

The English custom of storing wine underground in cellars was not suited to the climate or geographic conditions in New Orleans, since the city flooded regularly. Nor were there caves readily available in the French tradition. South Louisiana was hot, muggy, and moldy, features generally detrimental to the long-term storage of wine. In addition to these adverse storage conditions, the land and climate were not conducive to growing the appropriate grapes (*Vitis vinifera*). So colonists made wine from local grapes (*Cynthiana*) and from other fruits, but these wines were generally considered to be no more than satisfactory at best.

Imported wine became a sought-after commodity and a sign of wealth. New Orleanians of means poured their wine from glass decanters and consumed it in special glassware, often detailed with fine etching. Owning the correct accoutrements for wine drinking and knowing how to use them properly was a way to signal culture and prosperity to one's fellow drinkers.

Wine, however, is a delicate, living thing. It was not improved by the heat and jostling of the ocean journey to the New World. French wine was usually shipped in bottles packed in wooden casks filled with straw. The casks served as ballast, adding weight and stability to ships during their voyages. But bottles were fragile and often broke during the trip, resulting in a loss of product.

As England, France, and Spain jockeyed for power and influence in the New World, the often-tense political situation also complicated shipping. French and Spanish ships carrying wines to the Caribbean and on to the Gulf of Mexico and New Orleans were vulnerable to attack from English pirates and privateers, who seized cargoes whenever possible. Since many bottles were likely spoiled if they arrived in New Orleans at all, imported wines were an expensive gamble.

Hardier, fortified wines, however—such as sherry, port, and especially Madeira—could survive the hot and unsteady conditions inherent in a sea voyage to the New World. Madeira became the wine of choice in the American English colonies, largely because of European politics. Portugal, which controlled the island of Madeira off the coast of Africa, was an English ally, so Madeira was easily imported into the eastern colonies. Since New Orleans was a French and (after 1763) Spanish colony, importation of Madeira was far from natural or easy. But the taste for Madeira grew in New Orleans, since it not only survived the journey from the Old World, but also continued to improve in the city's hot conditions. Madeira merchants took advantage of local conditions to use less brandy in the fortification process of the product sent to Caribbean and Gulf ports, so that a New Orleans style of Madeira developed.

As the eighteenth century progressed, it became easier to obtain imported wine. With advances in shipping technology borne of frequent trips, the voyage across the Atlantic became shorter. French and Spanish wines thus became more readily available in New Orleans. And as a result, wine and its proper enjoyment became the subject of intellectual conversation. As with the ability to serve wines in the proper vessels, knowledge of the finer attributes of wine signified a person's high culture and discernment. The culture of wine thus helped to create a hierarchy in the field of eating and drinking, which was becoming an art form in France, including the part of New France that was la Nouvelle-Orléans.

NEW WORLD SPIRITS

Since the early settlers of New Orleans came from wine-drinking cultures, they preferred brandy—distilled from wine—to other spirits. As long as Louisiana was either a French or a Spanish colony, brandy was readily available, albeit expensive. Like unfortified wines, it had to be imported from Europe, since the right kind of grapes would not grow in Louisiana's hot and humid climate. Even though rum and whiskey were available, brandy was the spirit of choice.

BRANDY MILK PUNCH

—— Makes 2 drinks ——

2 ounces brandy

1 cup whole milk

Confectioners' sugar—between 1 and 3 teaspoons to taste

Whole nutmeg for grating as garnish

1. Pour all ingredients except nutmeg into a cocktail shaker filled with ice. Cover and shake vigorously for a minute or two until drink is frothy.

2. Strain into a short glass filled with crushed ice. Grate nutmeg directly over glass for garnish and flavor.

   You can make this with bourbon instead of brandy. The taste is different, but it is equally delicious.

Rum from the Caribbean islands was a popular alternative to brandy in the Crescent City's early days. The spirit was derived from sugar, which Christopher Columbus brought with him to the Americas. In the mid-seventeenth century, the French began growing sugarcane on Saint-Domingue (today's Haiti) and elsewhere in the West Indies. They also brought slaves from Africa to perform the hard labor that inevitably accompanied planting and harvesting the sugarcane, and then making the sugar.

Sugar is difficult to produce, and cane only grows where it is hot. When undertaken by hand—as in the colonial era—the harvesting process was backbreaking and painful. The sharp leaves of the cane cut and bloodied slaves' arms and bodies as they moved through the fields. Slaves used machetes or cane knives to cut the tall, hard sugarcane, often carrying it by hand from the fields to the mill. The cane was crushed by stone mills powered by other slaves or by animals. While pulling the wheel of the grindstone was arduous, placing cane on the stone was dangerous. Many slaves lost limbs as the wheel relentlessly turned, crushing their arms along with the cane.

Sugarcane juice spoiled quickly, so during harvesttime slaves worked through the night to ensure product freshness. Rum was made directly from the cane juice or from the molasses that remained after sugar was processed.

Caribbean merchants supplied rum, as well as cane juice and molasses, to New Orleans. In the eighteenth century, no establishment in the city produced rum commercially, although individuals doubtless made rum in home stills. Sugarcane was grown in south Louisiana from early in the colony's existence. Jesuit priests—part of the early contingent of settlers in New Orleans—planted sugarcane around 1751. They used it and its products as a sweetener and probably to produce tafia, which essentially was an unaged rum. (By this time, distilling from fermented molasses was a well-established technology.) Their successful experiment proved that sugarcane would grow in south Louisiana's hot and extremely damp climate. Thereafter, planters throughout the region grew sugarcane for household needs, including rum making. Initially, sugarcane was not considered to be a cash crop or viable export, as it was in the islands. In 1764 eighteen hogsheads of New Orleans tafia are documented in a shipment bound for France, but that amount hardly reflects large-scale commercial production.

When Louisiana's indigo crop could no longer compete successfully with indigo plantations that had sprung up in Central America, planters began to cast about for another commercial crop to grow. Jean Étienne de Boré had an indigo plantation partially situated on what is now Audubon Park in New Orleans. He was facing a difficult financial future if he maintained his traditional course of planting indigo, so he decided to gamble on a new crop. He made the highly speculative leap to sugarcane, selling his first crop in 1796. In doing so, de Boré relied on the advice of Manuel Solís, who had come to south Louisiana from the Spanish Indies, where sugarcane was being successfully grown and tafia was being made. Solís settled in what is now St. Bernard Parish and began his own experimental plantings with sugarcane. De Boré consulted with Solís in 1790, relying on Solís's technical knowledge and his cane plants to begin commercial production of sugar.

De Boré is often incorrectly described as the first person to granulate sugar, but he was really the first person in Louisiana to produce sugar commercially. He also had a distillery near his sugar house. De Boré's innovative risk paid off for him and for future sugarcane growers in Louisiana. Following his lead, Louisiana sugarcane farmers began producing sugar commercially. Like him, they almost always had a distillery on the premises to take advantage of even the sludge left over from the refining process. Much sugarcane was grown in what is now St. Bernard and Terrebonne Parishes. The largest refinery in North America, the Domino Sugar Refinery, today operates in the St. Bernard town of Arabi, overlooking the Mississippi River and less than a mile from the downriver city limits of New Orleans.

⟶ COLONIAL GOVERNANCE ⟵ AND ALCOHOL

The very earliest French ordinances governing taverns and cabarets are lost, but it is possible to back into them by reviewing court cases based on violations of the law. In 1726, for instance, just eight years after the founding of the city, the Superior Council recorded the case of one Dupont. This case involved the violation of selling alcohol during Mass on Sunday. Thus we may assume that an ordinance outlawing the sale of alcohol on Sunday existed and had been promulgated, allowing for council action.

After this case, little relevant judicial documentation exists until 1746. A police regulation from that year allowed for the licensing of six taverns, a canteen for French soldiers, and another canteen for Swiss soldiers. The regulation also allowed for the operation of six cabarets. The cabaret licenses were to be obtained at public auction, each going to the highest bidder; they had to be rebid each year. Records show that the auction yielded six successful bidders, both men and women, who paid between 715 and 795 livres for an annual license. This means that New Orleans would have had six cabarets, six taverns, a canteen for French troops, and a canteen for Swiss troops, all selling alcohol. According to the 1745 census, eight hundred white men and three hundred black men and women lived in New Orleans. (There is no record of how many white women lived in the city.) By the numbers, then, there was a drinking establishment for every 66th or 67th white man.

A city ordinance from 1751, as translated by contemporary historian of Louisiana Charles Gayarré (grandson of Étienne de Boré) stipulates the rules for taverns:

> The keepers of these six taverns are permitted to supply with wine or spirits no other persons than travelers, sick people, the inhabitants, and seafaring men; and this they must do with the requisite moderation. We forbid them to furnish these articles to a soldier, under the severest penalties, and to Indians and Negroes, under the penalty of paying a fine of ten crowns, of being sentenced to the pillory, and of forfeiting by confiscation all the wines and liquors found in the house and shop of the offender; and should there be a repetition of said offense, said offender shall be sentenced to the galleys for life.

The stiff penalties meted out to those who served alcohol to "Indians and Negroes" suggest that such sales were occurring, at least in some of the taverns. The ordinance also prohibited "retailing refreshments" on Sundays during divine worship, indicating the persistence of the violation that had landed Dupont in hot water back in 1726. The taverns were required to close at 9 p.m. each day. The tavern license was 300 livres, of which 200 livres went to the parish treasury and 100 livres went to relief of the poor. It is clear that the city treasury was being fattened by licensing fees and fines. It also seems that the tavern business was lucrative enough that the payment of such a hefty licensing fee was worth the investment.

A 1763 report by Attorney General Nicolas Lafrénière to the Superior Council complained about the "rear of the City," which contained unlicensed and thus illegal drinking houses. The proprietors of these establishments sold alcohol to people who should not be drinking and took payment in barter. Lafrénière claimed that slaves were stealing from their masters—handkerchiefs, empty bottles, or other things of value—and using these items to barter for drink, which made them unproductive and inadequately subservient. Moreover, he fulminated, the white men who ran these illegal drinking houses were not paying the requisite fees and thus were not contributing to the betterment and progress of the city. And because the liquor served in their establishments was unregulated, it was often adulterated and watered down, so legitimate customers were being cheated.

Lafrénière's indignant report would not have much effect; that same year, the French ceded control of New Orleans and its vast territory in what would become the United States to Spain. Many New Orleanians did not welcome their new ruler, and the initial years of Spanish governance were unsettled. But when Irish-born governor Alejandro O'Reilly arrived in the city in 1769, he successfully imposed Spanish authority during his brief six-month sojourn. Among other things, he promulgated regulations for the many shops that sold alcoholic beverages. His decree permitted the operation of six inns, increased the number of taverns to twelve, and allowed for six billiard parlors and a lemonade stand. In 1775, the Cabildo granted Pedro Moris and Raymond Escate a contract to oversee the taverns and issue their licenses. Moris was also tasked with uncovering and reporting unlicensed operations. To ensure that the men could make a profit, considering that they were required to post a bond and pay a license fee to the city, the Cabildo increased the number of permitted taverns to twenty-four. That number continued to grow, and by 1789 there were ninety-four licensed taverns. Women and free people of color were now allowed to hold tavern licenses. Running a tavern was a profitable-enough profession that there was a waiting list for licenses. Selling alcohol was a popular business and drinking alcohol was a popular pastime, and both activities proved lucrative for the Spanish government.

As New Orleans expanded in size—a fact reflected in the increased number of places that sold liquor—the growing availability of rum, brandy, wine, and locally made beer also allowed per capita consumption to increase. Still, there were restrictions on what could be sold in each type of establishment. Taverns could serve spirits but were limited to offering food that was pre-prepared or eaten raw: cheese, bread and butter, oysters, salad, and radishes. Taverns could not serve beer, cider, liqueurs, or syrups. Inns served beer and spirits only at meals or for drinking off-premises. Billiard parlors were allowed to serve beer and cider only. Violation of the license terms meant revocation of the license, which could then be given to someone on the waiting list. That threat was an excellent form of enforcement.

Just as the French had used license fees and fines to enrich the city, so did the Spanish. Limits on the number of legal establishments also made it possible to ensure municipal control, both to protect consumers and to enforce order. By 1792, in addition to license fees, taxes were being imposed on taverns. This indicates that despite what tavern keepers paid for their licenses, there was enough money to be made in the tavern business to reward both the proprietor and the government. On many occasions, despite official regulations—special closing hours, limitations on workers going to a tavern during work hours, and many other restrictions—the police were easily convinced to look the other way with small bribes. Few policemen seemed to have thought that violation of liquor laws was a serious offense. Neither the French nor the Spanish were ever successful in keeping slaves or Native Americans from drinking or being sold liquor.

THE CONVERGENCE OF
TWO CULTURES

Will republicans, who glory in their sacred regard to the
rights of human nature, purchase an immense wilderness for
the purpose of cultivating it with the labor of slaves?
—*Balance and Columbian Repository,* 1803

In 1803 President Thomas Jefferson purchased the territory of Louisiana from France, doubling the geographic area of the United States and gaining the port of New Orleans for the young nation. That agreement was formalized at a grand banquet that took place in the Sala Capitular of the Cabildo, the government building next to St. Louis Cathedral on the Place d'Armes (now Jackson Square). Pierre Clément de Laussat, governor of Louisiana for the short three weeks that France held the territory before turning it over to the United States, had first received Louisiana from Spanish governor Juan Manuel de Salcedo. It was Laussat who then transferred the keys to the city of New Orleans to its new American governor, William C. C. Claiborne.

During the banquet marking this event, the first ceremonial toast was to the United States and its president, Jefferson. The wine chosen to represent the United States was Madeira, which was available in New

Orleans and also favored by the wealthy in the United States. Next, Spain and its king, Charles IV, were toasted with wine from Málaga and the Canary Islands. There followed a toast to France and its leader, Napoleon Bonaparte, with wine from Champagne—a pink and a white. The final toast was made by raising a glass to Louisiana. Each person was allowed to choose his own wine to raise for this last toast. Not only did this ceremony mark the transition of ownership of Louisiana and New Orleans; importantly, it also signaled and perhaps celebrated the newly conjoined cultures of the Old World and the New World. Both the Europeans and the Americans understood these drinking customs. The act of raising a glass together was a mutually understood cultural act. In doing so, each of the officials present was asserting his country's heritage and honor, as well as marking a moment of commonality and good will.

After the Louisiana Purchase, Americans began to move into New Orleans in large numbers. This was the beginning of a cultural sea change for the people living in the city. Americans spoke English, and they were merchants who valued money and commerce more than culture. They were not all Roman Catholic. Their values and customs were different from those of the French, who became reluctant Americans overnight.

The Americans found a cosmopolitan city full of unfamiliar customs, exotic people, and a plethora of diverse food and drink. Travel guides of the period, as well as visitors' diaries and letters, tell of the wide variety of foods sold in the teeming French Market. Newcomers to the city were especially amazed by fruits from Latin America, liqueurs and brandies, and the plentiful bounty of the Gulf of Mexico.

The new residents were also struck by New Orleans coffeehouses. As coffee became less glamorous and more commonplace, local coffeehouses metamorphosed into places where men could go for an alcoholic drink or a substantial meal. And, like coffeehouses today, they were open early. Patrons would go regularly to the same coffeehouse, perhaps one near their workplace. They came to know the staff and the other regulars, turning the place into an informal clubhouse for conversation, newspaper reading, and the exchange of news and gossip. Americans began to visit these coffeehouses, sharing in the exchanges of news and culture, and drinking alcohol.

The Americans who flocked to Louisiana came from a tradition of fermenting all sorts of vegetation, including turnips and pumpkins. They flavored their beer with sassafras, pine, and spruce. They drank cider. And they drank distilled liquors such as rum, gin, and grain-based spirits. They were not wine and liqueur drinkers like the residents of colonial New Orleans. Perhaps unsurprisingly, native New Orleanians saw American drinking habits as coarse and undiscerning. The alcohol itself seemed to be more important than the flavor. But virtually all of the inhabitants of New Orleans, both old and new, were drinkers.

In 1812, Louisiana became the eighteenth state in the Union. Statehood brought even more people into New Orleans. Many of them worked in the port and in various professions necessary to support the growing metropolis, which was now trading freely with the entire United States. Not only were more people moving to the city as residents, but more travelers were visiting as well, whether as tourists or on business. As a result, more hungry mouths had to be fed and supplied with drink. Most boardinghouses did not provide all of the day's meals. Coffeehouses—which numbered nearly one hundred by this time—were a popular option for dining. Their early opening hours made them especially convenient for workers who had to be on the docks before normal breakfast times. And, of course, alcohol often accompanied these meals.

SHRUB

—— *Makes approximately 1½ to 2 cups* ——

A shrub is acidulated, sweetened fruit juice that can be drunk with water as a refreshing beverage or mixed with spirits for an even more refreshing drink. Of course, you can make a fruit vinegar from fresh fruit, but a nice shrub can be made with purchased apple cider vinegar that contains an active mother. You can make this recipe with pieces of peach, nectarine, or apricot, or a bit of each. Mixed berries also make a wonderful shrub. Or you can make a single fruit shrub.

1 cup washed fruit, cut into pieces

1 cup granulated sugar

Unfiltered apple cider vinegar, approximately 1 cup

1. Place fruit and sugar in a quart-size, self-closing plastic bag. After closing bag, squeeze fruit and sugar together to enhance release of juices. Place bag in refrigerator.

2. In a day or two, bag should be full of juice. Strain, mashing vigorously to obtain as much juice as possible. Use remaining fruit for some other recipe. (It can be added to yogurt or a smoothie.)

3. Add any undissolved sugar to juice. Measure juice. Add a like amount of vinegar. Stir or whisk liquid and sugar.

4. Place in a glass bottle with a lid or cork. Refrigerate. After 7 to 10 days, the shrub will have mellowed and is ready for mixing.

For a zesty variation, add peppercorns or vanilla bean.

A modern shrub drink would combine an ounce of shrub, 2 ounces of spirits, and an ounce of a friendly liqueur over ice. Mixed with sparkling water, it makes a lighter drink.

During this time, public drinking in cities was common throughout the United States. Even so, visitors to New Orleans remarked on this aspect of the city's culture. Henry B. Whipple, who would later become the first Episcopal bishop of Minnesota, noted very negatively the widespread drinking culture of the city during his visit in 1844. He wrote in his diary, "Drinking is an awful vice here." This criticism may not have been wholly deserved; already in 1790, the per capita consumption of liquor in the United States was over five gallons a year. Yet Whipple's condemnation has been oft-quoted as evidence of New Orleans as a heavy-drinking town.

Whipple might well have been taken aback by the many types of alcohol available in the city, starting with the abundance and varieties of wine. Wine was drunk throughout the day, starting with breakfast; many city houses of wealthy New Orleanians included wine storage. Newspaper advertisements hawked numerous wines, imported Scotch and Irish whiskeys, liqueurs and cordials, absinthe, eau-de-vie, brandy, and fortified wines such as port and Madeira. Rum was already readily available in the city; now rye gained in popularity as well, to suit the taste of the incoming Americans. Drinking was still considered a healthful practice, certainly more healthful than drinking water. And perhaps the liquor-loving reputation of New Orleans was simply a confusion of the openness of drinking with licentiousness. Certainly drinking could and did cause fights and public drunkenness, but the city was giving way to business and enterprise, which required some soberness of body and judgment.

❧ HOTELS ❧

New Orleans was beginning to find its bearings not only as a place of strategic importance near the mouth of the Mississippi River, but also as a bustling port city. Businesses, including many related to the import/export trade, put down roots and began to grow. The increasing numbers of travelers on business needed convenient and well-appointed places to stay. To meet this demand, large and luxurious hotels were established. The bars in these hotels became focal points for the drinking culture that was part and parcel of doing business in the city. And as hotels began to compete with each other for business travelers, they innovated with alcohol to attract patrons.

In 1799, Samuel Moore opened the Hotel d'Orleans, which is credited with being the first hotel in New Orleans. Several other establishments—including the Hotel des Étrangers and the Hotel Tremoulet—opened shortly thereafter, as the city became larger and more American. In 1825 the Marquis de Lafayette stayed at the Hotel des Étrangers; other notable guests there included Napoleon Bonaparte's physician. By the 1830s, the city was in full flower. One reason for this explosion of growth was financial policy: during this time, the Louisiana legislature chartered state banks that were empowered to issue currency and had the means to finance grandiose projects—often at great risk, but often with substantial success. Eventually the banks were unable to sustain their leverage, and the banking bubble collapsed. But the scheme left hotels in its wake, even if it also left ruined banks. Two of the most grand were the St. Charles Hotel and the St. Louis Hotel, and they competed with each other for the designation of the finest hotel in the city.

In the first half of the nineteenth century, New Orleans was informally divided on either side of the axis created by Canal Street. The downriver side of the street, which included the French Quarter and the developing *faubourgs* (neighborhoods) such as the Marigny, Esplanade Avenue, and Tremé, identified with the old regime. The upriver side of the street, whose grand thoroughfare was St. Charles Avenue, was predominantly American. Identification with one side or the other began to blur as time passed and the city became assimilated into the United States, but in the first few decades after the Louisiana Purchase, the cultural identification either upriver or downriver of Canal Street was strong. And the St. Charles Hotel, both by location and ownership, was clearly an American hotel. It was built by a then-famous architectural firm, Dakin and Gallier, whose architects also designed the Opera House and the Old State Capitol in Baton Rouge. Construction of the St. Charles Hotel was finished in 1837. After a rocky start, the building became an important place for business and social gatherings until it burned in 1851. It was rebuilt and continued its history of ups and downs until it burned to the ground in 1894.

In its heyday, the St. Charles Hotel served as a magnet for commerce. Around it were clustered boardinghouses, bars, and restaurants. The hotel's large dome served as a landmark and helped to make St. Charles Avenue one of the world's most famous thoroughfares. A sixty-foot bar attracted customers throughout the day and evening, and the wealthy on world travels came to live at the hotel for months at a time.

If the St. Charles was the gathering place for the business class, the St. Louis Hotel in the French Quarter was the gathering place for politicians. The St. Louis Hotel also boasted a dome, which marked the center of the building. The rotunda and a large adjoining vestibule became a commercial space, where all manner of auctions—including slave auctions—took place. The hotel burned in 1841 and was rebuilt with arcades, which allowed the public to watch the ongoing business transactions as a kind of spectacle, close to the city's other public spectacle—the French Market. The St. Louis's large open arcades also made its rotunda a perfect place for politicians to give speeches, which could be watched and heard by people seated in the hotel's banquettes. All political parties used the rotunda for rallies and announcements.

One of the St. Louis's innovations was the free lunch in its elegant saloon. Although during the day and evening nibbles such as bread and butter, radishes, pickles, cheese, or dried meat might be set out on the hotel bar, at lunchtime the fare was spectacular and plentiful. Patrons were plied with soups and ham or roast beef while they drank, keeping them out of the coffeehouses and cafés. The practice was so successful that it was adopted by other hotel bars. Competition between hotel saloons began to revolve around which one offered the most lavish free lunch.

The first manager of the St. Louis Hotel was Pierre Maspero. He was followed by a man named Alvarez, whose assistant was Joseph Santini. James Hewlitt succeeded Alvarez, and under his supervision the hotel began to hold balls, which became known across the country. In the early 1840s, the St. Louis Hotel held a glittering "bal travesti," which was attended by former U.S. secretary of state and presidential candidate Henry Clay. In 1845, the Louisiana legislature met in its ballroom. After the Civil War, the hotel was purchased by Louisiana, and the state legislature met there from 1874 to 1882. It was eventually torn down.

In his history of the Omni Royal Orleans Hotel, which is the successor to the St. Louis Hotel, author John DeMers repeats the myth that the cocktail was invented at the St. Louis. According to legend, the drink was served in an egg cup, known as a *coquetier,* which was later corrupted into the word *cocktail* by the city's English speakers who could not pronounce the French word. This story reflects the reputation of New Orleans as the cradle of drinking culture and as the exotic crucible of cuisine and cocktails.

In fact, the earliest documented definition of *cocktail* appears in the May 13, 1806, issue of the *Balance and Columbian Repository,* a Hudson, New York, publication. A cocktail was described as "a stimulating liquor, composed of any kind, sugar, water, and bitters—it is vulgarly called a bittered sling." This article appeared before the St. Louis Hotel opened, so obviously the creation story is apocryphal. But accuracy should not get in the way of the larger truth that the mythology reflects, that New Orleans contributed mightily to the invention of cocktail culture.

➤ JOSEPH SANTINI ◄

In 1833, Joseph Santini, an immigrant from Trieste, Italy, opened a coffeehouse on Gravier Street called Jewel of the South. Santini's experiments with cocktails had an influence on the drinking culture of New Orleans, both at his coffeehouse and subsequently at the bar of the Exchange Hotel (the original name of the St. Louis), where he retired as manager in 1869. At the Exchange Hotel he invented the Crusta, which introduced citrus juice into the traditional cocktail formula of spirits, bitters, sugar, and water. Santini's innovation was recognized by Jerry Thomas, who included the Brandy Crusta in his iconic 1862 bartenders' guide to cocktails. Modern cocktail historians such as Ted Haigh consider the Crusta the precursor of the Sidecar.

Aside from being a master drink maker, Santini was known for his generosity and aid to education. He not only provided for the education of his seven children, but also supported scholarship at their schools. For example, he paid for special medals in recognition of the best student in French and elocution at the school of one of his daughters. He was supporting one of his children's musical pursuits in France when he died in 1874.

CRUSTA
—— *Makes 1 drink* ——

By using a different spirit, the drink becomes a gin crusta or a rum crusta.

1 whole lemon or a small orange that fits snugly into a small wine glass

Granulated sugar

½ ounce lemon juice, plus additional for sugaring glass rim

2 ounces brandy

½ ounce simple syrup

Dash of Angostura bitters

1. Cut off top and bottom of lemon and hollow it out, reserving juice and leaving a wide band of peel.

2. Crust top of a small wine glass with sugar by moistening rim with lemon juice and then dipping it into sugar. The sugar will get hard and make a seal. The drink is named for this sugar crust.

3. Place the band of lemon peel snugly around inside of the glass, allowing peel to rise slightly above the glass rim.

4. Mix remaining ½ ounce lemon juice, brandy, simple syrup, and bitters together and shake over ice. Strain into prepared glass. Drink from the citrus band.

SIDECAR

—— Makes 1 drink ——

¾ ounce freshly squeezed lemon juice, plus
   additional for sugaring glass

1 teaspoon granulated sugar

1½ ounces light rum

¾ ounce Cointreau

1. Prepare a cocktail glass by rubbing rim with lemon juice and
   dipping it into sugar to coat the rim. Set glass in the refrigerator
   to chill.

2. Add ¾ ounce lemon juice, rum, and Cointreau to a cocktail
   shaker with ice. Shake well. Strain into chilled prepared glass.

The drinking culture in New Orleans included the belief that being asked to take a drink together was a leveling act. It was an arrogant insult to refuse, implying that one was too good to drink with the person making the invitation. Visitors to New Orleans remarked on the amount of business done over a drink in a saloon. There were hundreds of bars, one to be found close to almost any business; Carondelet Street was especially known as an area where one could find a drink. Politicians, too, used the power of drink to make their message sound more eloquent. If the word *lobbying* indeed comes from the practice of speaking in the lobbies of the legislative chambers, it really happened in New Orleans, when the Louisiana legislature met in the lobby of the St. Louis Hotel, so close to its famous saloon.

❧ PEYCHAUD'S BITTERS ❧

Early cocktails are still with us in the form of the Sazerac and the old-fashioned, both of which developed from the unbittered drink called a sling. New Orleanians still identify with and drink the Sazerac, which the city can legitimately claim as its own creation. And the city can also claim the invention of Peychaud's bitters. Pharmacist Antoine Amédée Peychaud is credited with formulating both.

At the turn of the nineteenth century, Peychaud arrived in New Orleans as a young man seeking refuge from the slave uprising in Saint-Domingue, then a French colony in the Caribbean and now the nation of Haiti. He became an apothecary and in about 1830 developed his own medicinal bitters formula. Bitters are made by steeping botanicals in alcohol, and mixology was a common practice for pharmacists in the first half of the nineteenth century. Peychaud's bitters were gentian root–based and are still produced today, and Peychaud is credited with being the first commercial developer of bitters in the New World.

According to legend, Peychaud added his bitters to cognac, which was the normal base for carrying aromatic medicinal bitters. The concoction was served in a *coquetier* with a little sugar and offered for various healthful purposes, such as curing intestinal illness and stomach disturbances. As absinthe's popularity grew, it was added as an ingredient, giving another level of complexity to the cocktail that would become known as the Sazerac.

While bitters are experiencing a renaissance today as part of the craft cocktail movement, Peychaud's bitters have survived for over a hundred years—a testament to the excellence of his bitters as well as the traditionalism of New Orleans.

⇝ ABSINTHE ⇜

One indication of a continued connection between New Orleans and Paris was the popularity of absinthe in both cities. With its high alcohol content, its ritual, and its mysterious ability to louche or become cloudy and greenish in color, absinthe was the drink of choice of the demimonde. Arthur Rimbaud, Edgar Degas, and Henri de Toulouse-Lautrec were among those on the Continent who were companions of *la fée verte*. Oscar Wilde and Edgar Allan Poe were known to consort with the Green Fairy, as absinthe was called. They and other bohemians enjoyed its so-called dangerous nature, feeling the *frisson* of naughtiness for drinking the stuff and experiencing its effects, basking in the disapproval of conventional society.

Absinthe gets its name from *Artemisia absinthium,* or wormwood,

The Old Absinthe Bar, founded in 1806, reputed to be the first saloon in New Orleans and the precursor to the Old Absinthe House. (Courtesy SoFAB Institute)

The Old Absinthe House, at the corner of Bienville and Bourbon Streets. Its legendary green marble absinthe fountains were once removed but have been restored and are on display there today. (Courtesy SoFAB Institute)

a silver-leaved, bitter, anise-flavored herb that had been used since the Egyptians as a vermicide. The spirit's green cast comes from a high amount of chlorophyll. Traditionally, it was drunk with a lump of sugar and water and with great ceremony. The paraphernalia and preparation rite no doubt added to absinthe's mystique and appeal.

A fountain with spigots was used to pour cold water in a controlled stream or to drip it slowly over a sugar cube. A decoratively pierced spoon held the lump of sugar over the drink glass, allowing the water to filter into the absinthe below. If there was no fountain, water could be slowly poured from a pitcher or a carafe. French cartoons make fun of the heights from which the water was poured to ensure a proper louche. The oils from the herbs that are macerated in the spirits (and that give the absinthe its flavor) dissolve in the alcohol. When there is sufficient water in the glass, the oils become cloudy and change color.

Although absinthe was available in many coffeehouses and saloons in New Orleans, the Old Absinthe House, at the corner of Bienville and Bourbon Streets, was graced with legendary fountains. Built in 1806, the building was used as a food wholesaler, an épicurie, and even a bootshop before it became home to Aleix's Coffee House in 1846, run by Jacinto Aleix and his family. Like other coffeehouses in the city, it served alcohol. Later, bartender Cayetano Ferrér began serving the popular Absinthe Frappé. In 1874 Ferrér, who had leased the place, renamed it the Absinthe Room. Later it was named the Old Absinthe House.

The building was nailed shut during Prohibition, and it remained dark. But the marble bar, the cash register, the familiar paintings, and the fountains were removed from the building by Pierre Cassebonne, who bought them to create the Old Absinthe House Bar up Bourbon Street. In 2004, the furnishings were returned to their original home, where they can be seen today. The most important features are the green marble fountains, each topped with a bronze figure and equipped with spigots for dripping. Notable features of these fountains are their extremely pitted limestone bases. Some explain the pitting as the result of gallons and gallons of water dripping drop by drop onto the limestone, eroding depressions into the surface. Others believe the pitting is too extensive to have been caused by the simple dripping of water. It is also speculated that the fountains may have been used as seltzer fountains. The acidic nature of the seltzer would have gradually eaten into the limestone, causing the pitted surface.

Because of health concerns associated with the compound thujone found in absinthe, the spirit was banned in the United States in 1912, and it was not again legal until 2007. Ted Breaux, an environmental chemist originally from New Orleans, reverse-engineered pre-ban absinthe. Breaux determined that absinthe made with wormwood contains only minute quantities of thujone. Thujone was considered toxic and was incorrectly thought to be responsible for the erratic behavior of some absinthe drinkers. Breaux determined that the government ban on absinthe was based on pseudoscience; he used real science, in the form of a mass spectrometer, to prove that thujone was not present in sufficient quantity in absinthe to have any deleterious effects. Breaux now produces his own line of absinthe at a distillery in Saumur, France.

Two New Orleans brothers, Ray and B. J. Bordelon, recently became fascinated with absinthe, as well as its paraphernalia. They love the taste of absinthe, and they have become historians of the drink and collectors of the special artifacts surrounding its ritual. In 2003, they created the Absinthe Museum in a shop on Royal Street. The shop closed in 2010, and the brothers reopened La Galerie d'Absinthe inside the Southern

Food and Beverage Museum. The exhibit is one of the largest collections of absinthe artifacts on display in the United States. The exhibit also educates museum visitors on the history of absinthe in New Orleans, including the famous people who imbibed the drink in the city, such as Mark Twain, Walt Whitman, and Lafcadio Hearn.

⟶ THE PRECURSOR OF THE SAZERAC ⟵

In recent times, the Sazerac has become the cocktail most associated with New Orleans. The Louisiana legislature adopted a resolution in June 2008 making the Sazerac the city's official cocktail. The original bill, filed by state senator Edwin R. Murray (D-New Orleans), proposed naming the Sazerac the official state cocktail, but some legislators felt that having a state cocktail would send the wrong message about Louisiana to the rest of the country. They compromised on New Orleans—which was only fitting, as the Sazerac was invented in the Crescent City.

The origins of the Sazerac can be traced to Sewell T. Taylor and Aaron Bird. Around the middle of the nineteenth century, Taylor sold his Merchant Exchange Coffee House to Bird and went into the liquor distribution business. One of the cognacs he sold was Sazerac-de-Forge et Fils. Bird began serving Taylor's cognac at his coffeehouse and made an eponymous cocktail with it, adding Peychaud's bitters and absinthe. Eventually he changed the name of his establishment to the Sazerac House. Over the next twenty years, the place was sold and passed along until Thomas Handy bought it in 1869 or 1870. Handy was an entrepreneur in the liquor industry. He obtained the rights to Peychaud's bitters in 1873. In the 1870s, because of an increase in the cost of cognac caused by the pesky disease of grape phylloxera, he began using an American spirit—rye whiskey—as the base liquor of the drink, although it continued to be called a Sazerac. Some cocktail historians argue that the drink was not really a Sazerac before it was made with rye. Handy bottled the drink, using rye, and sold it during the 1890s.

C. J. O'Reilly, at one time Handy's secretary, later established the Sazerac Company. Except for a hiatus during Prohibition, it has been in the distilling business ever since. One of the products the Sazerac Company acquired was Herbsaint. In the early twentieth century, when absinthe was banned by the U.S. Department of Agriculture, Herbsaint was substituted without serious change in the flavor profile of the Sazerac. In New Orleans, it is still the standard spirit used to provide the anise aspect to the drink.

Cocktail napkin from the Roosevelt Hotel, advertising the famous Sazerac. (Courtesy SoFAB Institute)

Indeed, the Sazerac richly deserves its designation as the official cocktail of New Orleans. The Sazerac brand of rye whiskey is owned by Buffalo Trace Distillery, which has New Orleans roots. Peychaud's bitters is now also owned by Buffalo Trace Distillery. With the addition of Herbsaint and sugar produced by the Domino Sugar Refinery in nearby Arabi, the Sazerac could not be more homegrown.

⇥ HERBSAINT ⇤

Herbsaint was first produced by J. Marion Legendre and Reginald P. Parker. It is said that Parker learned the recipe for absinthe when he was serving in Marseille during World War I. After returning to New Orleans, he began to produce the drink using the alcohol that pharmacy-owning Legendre obtained for medicinal purposes. The two made and enjoyed this drink during Prohibition. When they exhausted the supply of herbs Parker had brought back to New Orleans from Europe, Legendre imported them. In return, Parker gave Legendre the recipe. Legendre began selling Legendre Absinthe in 1934 after Prohibition was repealed. Although his absinthe never contained wormwood, the federal government required Legendre to change the name of his product. He chose the name Legendre Herbsaint. *Herbe sainte* was the French name for wormword.

Legendre was licensed as a rectifier almost immediately after Prohibition ended, allowing him to blend spirits and to produce liqueurs. In an interview given to Jay Hendrickson, a noted Herbsaint historian, Legendre explained that when he first began to make his absinthe, there were no facilities available for production. Although Prohibition was over, neither the federal nor the local government had established inspection and taxing mechanisms. The result was that he made his first batches of product in his attic. Later he manufactured Legendre Herbsaint at his offices, and finally in warehouses, where he could obtain more efficiencies. Herbsaint was a steady seller, but not a regular ingredient in most cocktails. The slightly licorice flavor was intensely distinct and not universally popular, although it sold well in New Orleans, and also in Chicago, San Francisco, and Los Angeles.

Legendre Herbsaint was blatantly and poetically advertised by the collector William B. Wisdom as a connection to European flavors that were part of the heritage of New Orleans. Although the product could not use absinthe in its name, its advertising referred to the flavors of absinthe, the traditional recipe, and family tradition while simultaneously reminding customers that it did not contain and never contained wormwood. The advertising campaign sought to evoke the spirit of absinthe while asserting the product's safety. Yet the drink still failed to catch on. Frustrated that even with a large advertising campaign Herbsaint did not become universally popular, Legendre sold his creation to Sazerac and Company in New Orleans. Today the Sazerac Company, now headquartered in the New Orleans suburb of Metairie, is the largest distiller in the United States. Not only does it still produce Herbsaint, but it owns many other distilling companies and brands of liquors.

Legendre's Herbsaint was not the only absinthe sans wormwood in the city. In 1934, a group of companies making absinthe-flavored drinks established the New Orleans Absinthe Manufacturers Association. They used the word *absinthe* in their name in spite of the ban on absinthe that had been put in place over twenty years earlier—testament to the city's lack of respect for authority, especially when the authority is thought to be wrong.

HERBSAINT FRAPPÉ

—— Makes 1 drink ——

2 ounces Herbsaint

1 tablespoon simple syrup

2 ounces sparkling water (unsalted is best)

1. Chill a thin 6-ounce glass by stirring crushed ice in it until the glass is frosted.

2. Mix ingredients over ice in a cocktail shaker to blend and cool. Strain into empty frosted glass.

ICE, THE SALOON, AND
THE EMERGENCE OF
THE CELEBRITY BARTENDER

In the eighteenth century, ice was a harvested product that only the wealthiest in the South could afford. Up north, George Washington and other American landowning notables built icehouses on their properties for the preservation of foods and medicinal purposes, not to cool drinks. Those who lived in colder geographical areas could harvest ice each winter and save it in the icehouse. In New Orleans and the warm climate of the Caribbean, that was not possible.

Harvesting ice from the frozen ponds of New England to send to Martinique was the wild idea of two brothers from Boston, William and Frederic Tudor. According to legend, the brothers talked about how to send ice to the Caribbean to cool the region's inhabitants during the summer. The idea resonated with Frederic, and he convinced his brother to go into business with him to ship ice to the Caribbean.

Their venture raised about $10,000 in capital. But Frederic had difficulty finding a ship that would take the ice as cargo—for fear of it melting and sinking the ship—so he used part of the capital to buy a vessel of his own. He filled it with ice and set sail for Martinique in 1806, but what was left of the ice upon arrival was not well received by the islanders.

After several abortive attempts to deliver ice to the Caribbean, Tudor hit on the idea of selling his ice in southern port cities of the United States—Savannah, Charleston, and New Orleans.

The first shipment of ice arrived in New Orleans in 1826. As the story goes, the city's mayor was afraid the ice would have a negative effect on the health of the citizenry and thus ordered that it be dumped into the Mississippi River. Even if this episode is apocryphal, such an attitude reflects a very European mindset and aversion to cold beverages. But despite any initial misgivings, ice was soon in demand in New Orleans.

Ice was outlandishly expensive, however, so Tudor used a marketing technique that overcame any initial reluctance about its price: he offered a first supply of ice for free to potential customers. This allowed bars to offer chilled drinks at the same price as room-temperature drinks. He predicted that once patrons had tasted a chilled drink, they would request more. And he was right. With demand established, more and more bars signed up for ice.

Following Tudor's success, competitors also began selling harvested ice. By the mid-nineteenth century, the family icebox was well established. The demand for ice was great enough that icehouses developed in larger communities. These houses resold ice purchased from larger harvesting establishments.

Whether shipped by train or water, ice was still costly cargo, as there was so much waste in transport. Savvy entrepreneurs began to think about a mechanical means of ice production, which would mean freedom from reliance on harvested ice. It would also mean that ice could be made independently of weather conditions. Inventors developed and patented several different types of machines. The first commercial mechanical ice facility in New Orleans, the Louisiana Ice Manufacturing Company, was established in 1868. This was actually the first large mechanical ice facility in the entire United States. It was located on Delachaise Street and was steam powered.

A commercial tug-of-war soon developed between the established ice sellers, who sold ice "made by God," and the new manufacturers of mechanically made ice. With increased industrialization came increased water pollution. People complained about the state of natural ice; it was no longer clean. Conversely, others were reluctant to use industrially produced ice because they were not sure if it was clean. Eventually, the efficiencies and improvements of mechanically produced ice made ice harvesting an obsolete industry.

Pelican Ice claims to be the oldest continuously operating ice company in North America. It began as the New Orleans Ice Company in 1870. Its original building had thick masonry walls insulated with cork and a high ceiling for stacking lots of ice. The company sold ice in 100-, 50-, and 10-pound blocks. Even at 25 cents for 100 pounds, many meat markets bought only enough ice to keep their meat cool during the day. These markets overnighted their meat in the ice facility itself rather than buy more ice for the night, establishing the practice of cold storage.

ICE AND THE COCKTAIL

New Orleans did not invent cocktails, and it did not invent ice. But when ice arrived, the city was ready to embrace it. In addition to its health and safety benefits in food preservation and medical use in treating fevers, ice meant refreshment in the heat of the subtropical climate. And alcoholic drinks could be improved in flavor and enjoyment.

Once ice was produced in quantities and at prices that allowed for its widespread use, the creativity of bartenders and the demands of the public made ice a medium of expression. Ice could be chopped off the block. It could be cracked into a size that would approximate today's ice cube. It could be crushed with a hammer into fragments. And it could be shaved into a fluffy, snowlike consistency. These various forms of ice created different qualities in an alcoholic drink. For example, when dilution was not desired, pieces of cracked ice could be added to a glass to chill a drink and then strained out as the drink was poured into a separate glass. Crushed ice could be used to slowly dilute and chill a drink, as with the mint julep. And shaved ice could almost instantly chill a drink and provide a cooling sensation during drinking, as well as a variable feeling in the mouth. All of these properties were crafted into the developing cocktail.

There were other factors besides a desire for refreshment and a practice of drinking alcohol that made the cocktail gain in popularity in New Orleans. Alcohol was enjoyed and accessible on many social and economic levels. The city had ample places in which to drink, and a variety of venues to choose from. For these and other reasons, the drinking of iced alcoholic beverages became an early cultural phenomenon in New Orleans. And to this day, New Orleans has held on to that cocktail tradition, as well as its cocktail reputation.

✦ RAMOS' ORIGINAL GIN FIZZ ✦

Henry Charles "Carl" Ramos, gentleman bartender, was the purported inventor of the eponymous gin fizz. Ramos was born in Indiana in

1856. His family moved to New Orleans when he was still a boy, and he was raised in the city. His early life is not well documented, and there is speculation about his early professional life. According to a story in the *Baton Rouge Advocate,* Ramos began his career in Baton Rouge, working at the Capitol Saloon. A friend of his, Philip Machet, owned and operated a package liquor store. Machet was an enterprising sort, and as a way to encourage business, he created a new drink from gin, cream, egg white, lemon juice, and soda water. He offered this mixture to customers each day in his store. The demand for Machet's drink began to outperform the demand for his package liquor, and he offered the recipe to Ramos in order to relieve himself of the obligation of preparing the daily refreshment.

Ramos left Baton Rouge and established himself in New Orleans in the 1880s. After tending bar at Sumpter House, he opened the Imperial Cabinet Saloon on Gravier Street and St. Charles, across the street from the St. Charles Hotel. He—not Philip Machet—is usually credited with inventing the gin fizz, originally called the New Orleans Gin Fizz, in 1888. Ramos employed a large number of bartenders—as many as twenty at a time—to make this drink for thirsty patrons. By one account, at Mardi Gras there were thirty-two bartenders, known as shaker boys, shaking the drinks. Because each drink takes longer to make than the usual cocktail, extra personnel were needed to keep up with demand.

Wherever he went, Ramos was admired for his gentlemanliness and his civic contributions. Regardless of whether he was the inventor or the successful promoter of the Ramos Gin Fizz, he is the person who made it famous. Ramos made a successful living from his gin fizz and the other drinks he sold, allowing him to give scholarships to worthy students. He was a temperate man and expected temperance and self-control of

Henry Charles "Carl" Ramos (*far left*), inventor of the eponymous gin fizz, and his staff at the bar of the Imperial Cabinet. (Collection of Chris McMillian)

his patrons. He believed in family and closed his bar early. He was a Freemason and abstained from drinking at some times in his life. But without irony or hypocrisy, he encouraged and supported the pleasure that others took from drinking.

Ramos resisted opening his bar on Sunday as so many other owners did in violation of the Sunday closing laws, although he did eventually succumb to the marketplace and open from 11 a.m. to noon and for another hour in the afternoon. Carrie Nation, that very strident destroyer of bars, did not harm Ramos's establishment when she came to New Orleans. According to the Ramos myth, she averred that if everyone who served liquor was like Mr. Ramos, there would be no need for the Prohibition movement. (Cocktail historians would all like to find that quotation reported in a contemporaneous newspaper. But the story still informs the character of Ramos, even if it cannot be confirmed.) Ramos

Ramos Gin Fizz ad, 1935. (Collection of Chris McMillian)

did close his bar during Prohibition. He would not be made a criminal, and he did not possess the cynicism that Prohibition brought out in the rest of the city. He died in 1928 and was of such national renown that his death was mentioned in *Time* magazine.

The "fizz" is a drink that includes spirits, a sour or acidic element such as lemon juice, and carbonated water. The gin fizz could be varied by the inclusion of additional ingredients, such as egg whites, whole eggs, sparkling wine, or, to make the Ramos Gin Fizz, cream and egg white. Ramos sold the recipe for the "one and only one" to the Roosevelt Hotel, which trademarked the name Ramos' Original Gin Fizz in 1935. The colorful and controversial Louisiana governor Huey P. Long often could be found at the Roosevelt enjoying the Ramos Gin Fizz. When Long moved to New York, he brought Roosevelt Hotel bartender Sam Guarino with him to ensure that the New Yorker hotel bar staff could produce a passable drink.

The Ramos Gin Fizz is still identified with New Orleans, and it is still popular in the city. It has a complex flavor and unique mouth feel. Like other drinks New Orleanians have embraced, this drink is a tangible link to the past. And it is also a drink that can appeal to sophisticated palates. Cocktail historian David Wondrich has suggested that New Orleans should abandon its love affair with the Sazerac and adopt the Ramos Gin Fizz as its signature drink.

The following recipe by bartender Chris McMillian contains vanilla. According to Chris, vanilla is thought to be a secret ingredient of the Ramos Gin Fizz. There is controversy about this; some people protest that there is no place for vanilla in the Ramos Gin Fizz. You may have to try it for yourself.

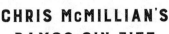

CHRIS McMILLIAN'S RAMOS GIN FIZZ

—— *Makes 1 drink* ——

2 ounces gin, preferably Old Tom

2 ounces heavy cream

1 egg white

1 ounce simple syrup (recipe opposite)

½ ounce lemon juice

½ ounce lime juice

3 drops orange flower water

2 drops vanilla

Crushed ice

Club soda, to top

1. Place all ingredients, except ice and club soda, into a shaker. Shake vigorously without ice for at least a minute to combine.

2. Add crushed ice to shaker and shake again for a minute or two.

3. Strain mixture into a chilled Collins glass without ice. (A fizz is always served without ice.)

4. Top up with club soda. A bit of froth can overflow down sides of the glass for effect.

SIMPLE SYRUP

—— Makes about 1½ cups ——

A syrup is part of the dilution of a drink, and using a syrup to sweeten and flavor a cocktail means that the sugar will be perfectly dissolved. There are two types of simple syrup—one that is a one-to-one ratio of sugar and water; and a sweeter version, often called rich syrup, that uses two parts sugar and one part water. Rich syrup allows for a lesser dilution of the cocktail.

1 cup water

1 cup sugar

1. In a medium, heavy-bottomed saucepan, heat the two ingredients together over medium temperature until sugar is dissolved, stirring constantly. Do not boil.

2. Cool completely. Bottle the syrup and refrigerate. Keeps up to one month.

The same technique with two cups of sugar makes rich syrup.

Variations of this syrup recipe can be made using citrus peel or herbs, such as mint or basil leaves. To make a flavored syrup, heat the sugar and water with the peel or herbs. Crush them with the back of a wooden spoon. Allow the syrup to cook and then strain out the solids. Bottle and store in the refrigerator.

THE ONE AND ONLY ONE
RAMOS' ORIGINAL GIN FIZZ

(1) One tablespoonful powdered sugar.

Three or four drops of Orange Flower Water.

One-half lime (Juice).

One-half lemon (Juice).

(1) One Jigger of Old Tom Gin. (Old Gordon may be used but a sweet gin is preferable.)

The white of one egg.

One-half glass of crushed ice.

About (2) tablespoonsful of rich milk or cream.

A little Seltzer water (about an ounce) to make it pungent.

Together well shaken and strained (drink freely).

To those who may have forgotten, a "jigger" is a stemmed sherry glass holding a little more than one ounce.

❧ RYE ❧

The main source of revenue of the fledgling United States was the government tax on imported goods. The personal income tax was over a century away. And, like Americans today, early citizens made economic decisions—including decisions about what to drink—based on value.

A common spirit at the time was rye whiskey. Rye was not taxed because it was made in America from an American grain. In contrast, wine was primarily an imported product and therefore was heavily taxed. In addition to being expensive, wine had an alcohol level much lower than that of rye. Thus rye delivered a bigger kick for less money. Obviously rye represented the better all-around value.

A misbegotten attempt to impose an excise tax on domestic liquor, the infamous Whiskey Tax of 1791, met with widespread resistance and was repealed in 1801. New Orleans did not become part of the United States until 1803, and thus it was spared the controversy surrounding the Whiskey Tax. After the Louisiana Purchase, the U.S. government tried to impose taxes on imported wine and liquor, in accordance with American law, but the city's proximity to the Gulf of Mexico made it easy for smugglers to bring in wines and spirits. New Orleanians continued to drink wine and brandy, but rye gradually became a popular—and much cheaper—alternative.

❧ THE WHISKEY COCKTAIL AND ❧ THE OLD-FASHIONED

The whiskey cocktail was often made with rye, sugar, water, and bitters. As time passed, it became a more common drink. It was widely sold, made with various spirits, in New York in the 1830s. As the nineteenth century progressed, the drink changed and its ingredients were varied. Indeed, it changed so much that the simple, original drink became known as the old-fashioned.

New Orleanians may not have been early rye enthusiasts, but the liquor did eventually catch on. In 1884 and 1885, many tourists traveled to the city for the World Cotton Exposition. Journalist and New Orleans observer Lafcadio Hearn published a cookbook for those visitors called *La Cuisine Creole,* which contained some of the special foods that have made New Orleans famous, such as gumbo and jambalaya. It also included recipes for drinks then being enjoyed in New Orleans, suggesting that drinking cocktails was an essential aspect of the city's culture.

Here is the recipe for the whiskey, brandy, or gin cocktail from *La Cuisine Creole:*

> Two dashes of Boker's, Angostura, or Peychaud bitters—either will make a fine cocktail. One lump of sugar, one-piece of lemon peel, one tablespoon of water, one wineglassful of liquor, etc., with plenty of ice. Stir well and strain into a cocktail glass.

The old-fashioned, when made with rye, is not as sweet as the drink made with bourbon. That is also true about the Sazerac. Most Sazerac recipes today call for rye.

Chris explains that despite the claim of the Pendennis Club in Louisville, Kentucky, to have invented the old-fashioned, it more likely originated from the frequent request of customers that a cocktail be made in the old-fashioned way, without new ingredients.

The old-fashioned is a built cocktail. It is built in the glass, not shaken and then poured into the glass.

CHRIS McMILLIAN'S
OLD-FASHIONED

—— *Makes 1 drink* ——

One sugar cube

5 drops of Angostura bitters

1 tablespoon water

1 piece fresh orange peel

Ice

2 ounces spirits

Cherry, orange slice, cocktail pick, and swizzle stick for garnish

1. Place sugar cube, bitters, and water in an old-fashioned glass and muddle them together until sugar is completely dissolved and liquid is clear. (Chris prefers to use a cube of sugar and water instead of simple sugar so that he can control the dilution.) Add orange peel and muddle again to release the oils.

2. Fill the prepared glass with ice. Pour spirits over ice.

3. Spear cherry and orange slice onto cocktail pick for garnish. Serve with swizzle stick. Each sip will change as the ice melts and affects the dilution of the drink.

Today, there are variations of the old-fashioned using many different spirits, from tequila to rum. But the principles are the same: spirits, water, sugar, and bitters. The cocktail.

CRESCENT CITY BITTERS

—— Makes about 2 cups ——

2 cups of overproof spirits* (bourbon is a good base)

5 whole cloves

2 cinnamon sticks, about 3 to 4 inches long

10 cardamom seeds

2 bay leaves

½ teaspoon of gentian root

5 dried sassafras leaves

2 cups pecans, toasted

1 tablespoon black peppercorns

5 dark-roasted coffee beans

2 tablespoons cane syrup

1. Mix all ingredients except cane syrup in a large jar. Cover and keep in a cool, dark place for two weeks. Shake every other day.

2. Strain solids through cheesecloth and reserve. Reseal alcohol in a clean jar and keep in a cool, dark place.

3. Bring a cup of water to a boil in a nonreactive pot. Add reserved solids to water. Reduce heat and simmer 12 minutes.

4. Allow mixture to cool. Strain through cheesecloth and reserve liquid. Discard solids.

5. Combine alcohol mixture and water mixture. Strain again.

6. Stir in cane syrup. Store in a dark glass bottle.

*"Overproof spirits" is the term used to describe distilled spirits that are stronger than the typical 80 proof standard.

CRESCENT CITY COCKTAIL

—— Makes 1 drink ——

1 teaspoon simple syrup

2 drops Crescent City Bitters (recipe opposite)

2-inch piece orange peel

2 ounces brandy

1. Mix syrup and bitters in a cocktail glass. Add ice and stir to chill glass.

2. Rub rim of glass with orange peel and squeeze peel into glass to add oils.

3. Add brandy. Stir and serve.

A julep was originally a rose-flavored preparation. The word derives from the Persian word *gulāb,* which means rosewater; over time, it came to refer to a flavored syrup. Juleps were once used for medicinal purposes as well as recreational drinking. Most often, a brandy or rum formed the base of the drink, depending on where the julep was served. Gradually, brandy was replaced with spirits made in America.

The mint julep is closely associated with the American South, especially when flavored with spearmint. Early accounts of julep ingredients did not include ice, leading cocktail historians to believe that it was originally served at the temperature of the liquids. But using cool spring water or well water could help raise the refreshment value of the drink beyond the cooling sensation of the mint.

The Mississippi River and its tributaries provided many opportunities for the exchange of culture between Americans and New Orleans around the time of the Louisiana Purchase. However crudely mercantile the Americans might have seemed to the cosmopolitan residents of New Orleans, the Americans brought with them some drinking practices that could be embraced, including the mint julep. Its ingredients—brandy, bourbon, or Kentucky whiskey, plus water, sugar, and mint—were readily available in the city, and it became part of the spirited canon of the city.

While its development is not precisely documented, the mint julep was a beverage particularly enjoyed by state and federal government officials in the nineteenth century. Favorite senatorial recipes have been memorialized.

Drinkers held the traditional julep cup of silver or pewter with flared sides by the edges to allow condensation to refreeze and frost the outside of the cup without being warmed by the hand. This added to the drink's refreshment value. Early references to the mint julep describe its base spirit variously as brandy or bourbon. Today, however, the mint julep is associated with bourbon or Kentucky whiskey. It became the official cocktail of the Kentucky Derby in the early twentieth century.

Chris McMillian can wax poetic about the mint julep. He has treated his patrons to the art of the layered mint julep, a built drink that is not stirred, in New Orleans and around the world. The taste of this layered version changes with each sip; as the ice melts, the syrup and the bourbon combine, and the mint spreads through the liquid. He treats the mint gently, explaining that mint is a delicate herb. Gentle rubbing or a quick clap between the palms can release the oils from the leaves, allowing the refreshing aroma to escape the cells of the leaves. The oils volatilize and escape quickly. But overly enthusiastic muddling will release not only the fragrant oils but also the chlorophyll, which is bitter. And the use of too much simple syrup can make the julep so sweet that it can hurt your teeth.

A mint julep is a drink to be sipped and enjoyed. And that means that it should be prepared with attention. In the traditional manner, Chris fills a heavy cotton canvas sack (a Lewis bag) with ice and pounds it with a wooden mallet to a proper crush. He fills a julep cup with the crushed ice, mounding it generously over the top of the cup, which contains three to six leaves of gently muddled mint. Next he adds the bourbon. By pouring it over the crushed ice, he creates an opportunity for the bourbon to chill as it percolates through the ice. Then he adds a bit of simple syrup. By the time he is ready for the garnish, the ice mound has collapsed into the glass. Finally, he garnishes the drink with a sprig of mint that he has clapped between his palms to release the fragrance. He does not stir the drink, but each sip is nevertheless redolent with the fragrance of fresh mint.

MINT JULEP
—— Makes 1 drink ——

3–6 fresh spearmint leaves, plus a sprig for garnish

Ice

2 ounces bourbon

1 ounce simple syrup

1. Place mint leaves in bottom of a chilled julep cup and muddle gently.

2. Place ice in a Lewis bag or wrap in a clean dishtowel. Crush ice with a mallet. Fill julep cup with ice until it mounds generously above top of cup.

3. Pour bourbon and simple syrup over mounded ice.

4. Clap mint garnish between your palms. Place it in side of cup in the ice. Serve immediately.

STORYVILLE
AND THE TOURISM OF
SEXUAL LICENSE

Order of the Garter: *Honi soit qui mal y pense*
(Shame to Him Who Thinks Evil of It)
—Motto of Storyville, reproduced on Blue Book covers

ineteenth-century New Orleans was a town prone to sexual license, and authorities increasingly tried to limit the areas where prostitution and other vices were tolerated. In 1857, the city began to impose licensing fees on prostitutes and their madams. The fees raised money for the city, and the license requirement allowed authorities to identify who was a working prostitute. Laws also prohibited women of color and white women from living and operating in the same houses, and prostitutes were barred from accosting potential customers on the street. Despite these measures, however, the sex trade flourished in the Crescent City.

⇸ GALLATIN STREET ⇷

In the mid-nineteenth century, the bawdy business of New Orleans was mainly conducted on Gallatin Street, near the French Market and the U.S. Mint, and close to the Mississippi River. (The open flea market pavilion of the French Market now operates where Gallatin Street used to be.) Bordellos, gambling houses, and bars crowded cheek by jowl on the tiny two-block street, whose residents plied their trades along with other businesses operating along the river. The street was named in honor of Albert Gallatin, who served as secretary of the treasury under Presidents Thomas Jefferson and James Madison, and who was instrumental in negotiating the Treaty of Ghent, which ended the War of 1812. Gallatin was not known to have a licentious nature, and it is ironic that his name is now strongly associated with vice in New Orleans.

The rowdy district was considered dangerous even for police, who often refused to set foot there. John Churchill Chase wrote of Gallatin Street that between 1840 and 1870 it was the "bawdiest, filthiest, wickedest two blocks in any community anywhere." Gallatin Street was ruled by the bellicose prostitute Mary Jane Jackson, also known as Bricktop because of her red hair. She was said to be able to fight anyone, man or woman, and is thought to have killed at least four people. She stabbed many of her victims with a special knife she always carried. According to her reputation, she had never backed down from a fight and had never lost one, either.

Gangs, which were often hired by business owners to vandalize competing businesses, controlled Gallatin Street. Fighting was a serious pastime, often resulting in death. The street was not an officially sanctioned vice district; it was a spontaneous and de facto area operating close to the action of the river, where rough and strong keelboaters and bargemen disembarked from journeys and looked for a little action. The legendary physical strength of the keelboaters increased the danger of fights. Around 1900, city authorities finally succeeded in cleaning up the district by tearing down the houses on one side of the street.

The French Quarter was also an area of carousing. Many tourists who came to New Orleans for the 1884 World Cotton Exposition found their way to the Quarter, and in particular to the nightlife on Royal Street. Accounts of open drinking, music, gambling, and prostitution abound. By that time, the more sober members of the city government were moving toward the idea of officially limiting prostitution and gambling (which was legalized in 1869). They believed that these activities would go on despite any attempts to prohibit them, so it would be more practical to simply corral the vice trades into a special, well-defined area. That way, people not interested in those activities could avoid them, and legitimate commerce could flourish outside of the vice district.

✣ STORYVILLE ✣

That new area was named Storyville, colloquially known as "the District." It existed for only about twenty years, but it had a great impact on the culture of the entire nation, incubating musicians who later played around the United States and the world, as well as other artists, most notably the photographer E. J. Bellocq.

Storyville got its name from New Orleans city councilman Sidney Story, who introduced the ordinance that established the defined area of vice. If areas of prostitution were limited to particular areas, he argued, they could be monitored in the same way as the red-light districts of Amsterdam and Hamburg. Port cities such as New Orleans inevitably tended to attract the sex trade, and he and others believed that creating such a district was preferable to having it pop up on its own without regulation—Gallatin Street being an example of just such an area.

The movement to create such a district was led by Mayor Walter C.

Basin Street, New Orleans, La.

BASIN ST.
"DOWN THE LINE"
NEW ORLEANS

Two views of Basin Street, one of Storyville's defined boundaries. *Down the Line* [bottom] shows the corner with Tom Anderson's Arlington Annex. [*Up the Line* courtesy Louisiana Division/City Archives, New Orleans Public Library; *Down the Line* courtesy Hogan Jazz Archive, Tulane University]

Flower. Ordinance number 13032, which authorized the district, read as follows: "From the first of October 1897, it shall be unlawful for any public prostitute or woman notoriously abandoned to lewdness to occupy, inhabit, live, or sleep in any house, room, or closet without the following limits: South side of Customhouse (now Iberville) from Basin to Robertson street, east side of Robertson street from Customhouse to Saint Louis street, from Robertson to Basin street." Interestingly, the ordinance did not authorize any particular activity in the newly created district. The politicians wanted to make clear that they were not condoning vice, but merely containing and controlling it.

The district consisted in part of grand establishments, sometimes called "sporting palaces," which were appointed with splendid amenities. Then there were shacks, known as "cribs," which were barely the size of a closet and existed in the run-down area behind the palaces. The cribs were located on Custom House (now Iberville) Street. Prostitutes plied their trade at the different levels of accommodations, charging accordingly. Both black and white prostitutes worked in Storyville, where black men were barred as customers. Black male patrons were allowed in an area adjoining the official Storyville, which was tolerated by the police. The open crossing of racial barriers in Storyville was a large part of its appeal and contributed to its reputation of wantonness.

Blue Books—directories of working prostitutes in the district, with descriptions of their talents, locations, and prices—were openly published, supported by advertisements, and available to visitors seeking these services. The motto of Storyville was printed boldly in every Blue Book, admonishing "shame to him who thinks evil of it." It was a direct challenge to the hypocrite. The Blue Book ads were primarily for nearby restaurants and music halls and for various liquors. During its heyday, the district also supported two newspapers that touted the doings in Storyville. The *Mascot* even boasted a society column that detailed the local goings-on, naming visitors and social activities. The *Sunday Sun* soon followed suit with its own society column.

Up to three thousand prostitutes operated in the district during the high season, which coincided with horse-racing season. The average number of prostitutes in Storyville at any time was about seven hundred. During Mardi Gras, the district was filled with revelers in costumes and masks.

Storyville was a place of music. Many larger houses hired piano players and jazz musicians. Buddy Bolden, Jelly Roll Morton, Louis Armstrong, and King Oliver were often seen in Storyville. Gertie Livingston, Josie Arlington, Lulu White of Mahogany Hall, and May Tuckerman were famous madams who were influential in the city during the district's heyday. Mae West famously performed the role of Lulu in the movie *Belle of the Nineties*.

Although sex was the primary commodity in Storyville, the sale of alcohol made the highest profits for entrepreneurs running the establishments. Sex was the lure, but liquor was the bread and butter. Absinthe, bourbon, and other drinks popular at the time were available in great quantities. Alcohol decreased inhibitions and helped get celebrations rolling. Like Gallatin Street, Storyville has been romanticized. Bellocq's photographs, which seem so romantic and haunting today, tell a grim tale of women trapped in a dead-end life of danger and hopelessness. The music and culture that developed in Storyville came at a price. And alcohol helped to make Storyville's denizens forget the price.

Vice continued to grow in New Orleans along with the population, moving its tentacles out from Storyville toward the river. Decatur Street was full of prostitutes opportunistically doing business with people disembarking from riverboats. The streets from North Rampart into the French Quarter were also walked by prostitutes as they informally extended the boundaries of Storyville. As the city expanded, conventional society began to feel Storyville's intrusion. Instead of a place where prostitution was hidden away out of sight, the district began to be too obvious a reminder of rampant licentiousness.

In 1908, a new terminal rail station opened at Basin and Canal Streets, only a block from Storyville. New Orleans–bound passengers found themselves greeted by partially clad or naked women, who waved from their windows at the trains. Popular outrage over such sights increased local support for the end of Storyville. The federal government wanted the district closed as well, claiming that it was a public health menace for soldiers mustering in New Orleans who were about to leave the States for service in World War I. Jean Gordon, a leading citizen, vociferously opposed the district. Although city officials did not want to close Storyville, finding it a convenient way to regulate prostitution, in the end they capitulated to outside pressure. The district was officially closed in October 1917. But an official decree did not mean the end of prostitution within its boundaries, with the larger houses continuing as speakeasies and places of entertainment.

These establishments were raided many times during Prohibition, yet they continued to operate. Frank LaMothe's restaurant, for example, became a speakeasy during Prohibition. LaMothe was also a music and entertainment promoter and general habitué of Storyville. Tom Anderson, a state legislator, was known as the "mayor of Storyville." Anderson ran several restaurants that advertised in a publication titled

SHERRY COBBLER

—— *Makes 1 drink* ——

4 ounces dry sherry

3 orange slices

2 teaspoons castor sugar

Mixed berries for garnish

1. Place sherry, orange slices, and sugar in a cocktail shaker with ice. Shake well.

2. Pour with ice into a glass and fill glass with mixed berries. Serve with a straw.

    A cobbler can be made with wine, making a pleasing drink for those who prefer wine's lower alcohol content.

the *Southern Buck*. His main establishment was called the Arlington Annex. Although Anderson did not openly run a bordello, his *Southern Buck* advertisements were ambiguously suggestive.

In 1937, after Congress passed the U.S. Housing Act, the city razed the remains of Storyville to build public housing. The "black Storyville" was located where City Hall is today.

⟶ PLAÇAGE ⟵

Many people confuse the system of plaçage with prostitution. While in some ways the two were related, they were not the same thing. In a plaçage relationship, a white man chose a woman, almost always of mixed race, with whom he set up a home, supporting her and their children. Frequently, the man also had a legal wife. The kept women, or placées, were often educated in womanly skills such as embroidery and singing, in order to present themselves as more attractive and re-fined. This arrangement was common with men who lived outside New Orleans, such as plantation owners. They lived with their legal wives at their plantation homes but would stay with their placées when they came to the city. But the institution of plaçage was by no means limited to men from plantations.

The laws of plaçage protected women who lived in "open concubi-nage" with a man, often taking his last name and in other respects acting as married. The placée was protected by law insofar as she was allowed to inherit from her partner, although offspring of the relationship were disadvantaged in contrast to "legitimate" offspring. Girls born of these relationships were often groomed for display at quadroon and octoroon balls, beginning the cycle of plaçage again. Male children were more problematic. Sympathetic fathers might send their sons to France to be educated and to live freely. In New Orleans, no matter how educated, such boys would probably become tradesmen.

While placées in many respects were disadvantaged and dependent women, they were not considered prostitutes, although they were scorned by women in legal marriages. Surviving accounts of placées often stress their beauty and feminine attainments. Since most marriages were arranged for business purposes, men chose their placées as love matches. In short, the institution of plaçage was a practical response and move to regulate an existing accepted practice.

Over decades, laws and attitudes toward mixed-race marriages, illegitimacy, and other social mores changed to make the practice of plaçage socially unacceptable and eventually obsolete. But accounts of quadroon balls and the custom of plaçage fueled the reputation of New Orleans as a place of sexual license, and subsequent activities in Storyville and on Bourbon Street only promoted that reputation.

❖ MILNEBURG, THE WEST END ❖ AND SPANISH FORT

When transportation was by foot or horse-and-buggy, a trip to Lake Pontchartrain from the French Quarter was a long outing. The shore of the lake was swampy, and the actual shoreline was not always well defined. As a result, much lakeside construction was done on piers that allowed the water to rise and fall under buildings. This also enabled houses to catch breezes over the water and made them seem exotic. Resorts developed along the southern shore of the lake, where Native American tribes once had settlements.

Much of the cargo and many of the people arriving in New Orleans in the nineteenth century came by way of Lake Pontchartrain and not up the Mississippi River. The journey from Mobile and other Gulf of Mexico ports was easier through the lake rather than up the mouth of the Mississippi. Trains connected the lake and the river, carrying cargo as well as people into and out of the city. With several trains offering daily service, small resort areas developed along the lakeshore, notably Milneburg, the West End, and Spanish Fort. In the summer, people sought entertainment as well as relief from the heat of the city, and many made their getaways to the lake resorts that were a mixed bag of hotels, restaurants, dance halls, bars, and amusement parks.

By the end of the nineteenth century, cargo ships were too large to use the shallow Lake Pontchartrain route and were thus limited to travel on the Mississippi River. At that point, the trains became almost entirely pleasure transports, taking vacationers to the resorts.

The West End, which began to be developed as early as the 1830s, was slightly farther west of Milneburg on the shore of Lake Pontchartrain. Originally called the New Lake End, in the 1880s it became known as West End. This area had buildings constructed on piers over the water, each with a boardwalk leading to the door of the establishment. During Prohibition, the limited access was a convenient way to delay the police if gambling, drinking, or other illegal activities were taking place inside.

The anchor of the West End was the West End Hotel. It had a huge saloon with a double bar and served many a resort-goer. In those days, there were no stools at the bar; it was manly to stand. Consequently, contemporary photos show men poised around the bar, each with a foot resting on the brass foot rail. When the West End Hotel burned in 1898, its demise was covered by the *New York Times*.

The West End boasted the third-oldest restaurant in New Orleans after Antoine's and Tujague's. Bruning's was opened in 1859 by Theodore Bruning, a German immigrant, and went through a number of incarnations. In the beginning it catered to adults, with drinking and gambling. Over the years, as more people had automobiles and the area became more accessible, its restaurant became more important than its resort activities. Bruning's finally became a family seafood restaurant known for its broiled trout, though it also had a large adjoining bar. After serious damage by Hurricane Georges in 1998, Bruning's abandoned its building on piers over Lake Pontchartrain and moved into a nearby structure at the water's edge. In 2005, however, the floods following Hurricane Katrina closed Bruning's forever. Its bar was rescued by the Southern Food and Beverage Museum and installed as a functioning bar in the restaurant Purloo.

Founded in 1849, the Southern Yacht Club (SYC) put down roots in the West End in 1857 so that members could use Lake Pontchartrain as a regatta playground. In 1879, the SYC built a clubhouse at the West End, and in 1899 the construction of an even bigger clubhouse led to more elaborate social activities and regattas. In 1949, the clubhouse was rebuilt into a modern structure. It, too, was a casualty of Hurricane Katrina, burning in the wake of the flooding. The SYC's current building was completed in 2009.

As the city extended out toward Lake Pontchartrain, a resort flourished at the West End where the New Basin Canal connected with the lake, complementing the businesses that were already there. A railroad was built along the path of the canal to connect the resort to the city. There was an amusement park and boat rides. In the 1920s, the amusement park was raised as a consequence of land reclamation efforts around the lake. The area was known for its seafood restaurants and bars. In addition to outdoor concerts, silent movies were screened at the resort.

In the 1830s, a resort was developed and was known as Milneburg, named after Alexander Milne, the area's principal landowner and investor. Milneburg, with its restaurants, hotels, and bars built on piers over the water, was initially considered to be far outside of town. To make the distance seem shorter, in the 1930s the Pontchartrain Railway, affectionately called the Smoky Mary, was built. The train connected New Orleans to Milneburg from the Mississippi River to Lake Pontchartrain, roughly the route of what is now Elysian Fields Avenue. The railroad tracks were extended out over the water to a dock, which allowed vessels to moor there and passengers to disembark. Those passengers could then board the train to New Orleans.

The Smoky Mary was a successful venture that brought people from the city to Milneburg. The landing, known as Port Pontchartrain, became a resort area with restaurants, bars, hotels, and bathhouses. A chain of boardwalks connected the buildings both to the shore and to each other. Over time, Port Pontchartrain began to lose importance as a commercial port. But Milneburg continued to be a popular resort, with "camps," the many small buildings built out over the water, available for rent for parties and fishing. During the 1930s, jazz bands and other musicians played at the Milneburg dance halls, honky-tonks, and camps. Thumbing their nose at the law, most bars and dance halls sold drinks, taking full advantage of being relatively far from the city and the authorities.

There was one more resort area trying to take advantage of lake breezes, Spanish Fort. In 1779, the Spanish had built a fort at Lake Pontchartrain—San Juan del Bayou—to protect the city from invasion from the north by water. After the Louisiana Purchase, the U.S. government in 1808 enhanced the fort's fortifications in order to protect New Orleans from northern intrusion. And in 1815, troops were posted there during the Battle of New Orleans to protect the city from that direction.

In 1823, the U.S. government sold the fort to Harvey Elkins, who constructed a hotel on the site. Spanish Fort began to be known as a resort area, although it was never as completely developed as the amusement areas at the West End or Milneburg. The hotel was eventually sold to John Slidell, who later sold the land he had accumulated. In 1877, Moses Schwartz purchased the area and built a theater and amusement park. An opera company produced summer performances at the theater, and before it burned down, Oscar Wilde also lectured there.

Starting with vagabonds and petty criminals, New Orleans has been built on a rough and uncourteous social foundation. From that beginning, with the overlay of American ingenuity and commercialism, the desire for pleasure has always lubricated the city's culture. Thus music, sexual license, and drinking could not be confined to one area or—as we shall see—eliminated by one puritanical legal gesture. They remain everywhere as a part of the spirit of the city, whether by the river or the lake.

PROHIBITION

OLD MAN BARLEYCORN BURIED IN FLOOD OF LIQUOR; NEW YEAR
GREETED BY BIG CROWDS IN RESTAURANTS AND STREETS
—*New Orleans States* headline, January 1, 1920

Prohibition, the "noble experiment," lasted from 1920 to 1933. The nationwide ban on alcohol began in 1917, when the U.S. Congress adopted the Eighteenth Amendment, making it illegal to manufacture, sell, or transport alcohol. But for the amendment to become effective, it needed ratification from two-thirds of state legislatures. By 1919, 36 of the then-48 states had done so, Nebraska being the state to bring the vote to two-thirds. Congress then passed the National Prohibition Act, commonly known as the Volstead Act, to carry out the intent of the new amendment and to define "intoxicating liquors" and provide penalties. Prohibition became law on January 16, 1920.

Despite New Orleans's reputation as a drinking haven, Louisiana was one of the states that ratified the amendment. The initial vote failed in the Louisiana Senate with a tie of 20–20. But in August 1918, a second vote shifted in the amendment's favor, making it 21 for and 20 against. No other state had such a close ratification vote. The Louisiana House of Representatives followed suit by approving ratification. In both cases, support for the amendment came from legislators from north Louisiana, which was largely Protestant, reflecting its English heritage. Roman Catholics lived mostly in the southern part of the state, which was settled by continental Europeans. The "dry" rural north and "wet" urban south often were, and to some extent still are, in a tug-of-war over the social and cultural mores of Louisiana.

If Prohibition's purpose was to stop the consumption of alcohol, the measure certainly did not succeed in New Orleans, where people defiantly continued to drink. During Prohibition, about five thousand commercial establishments served alcohol, marking the city as a place where alcohol was not only tolerated, but enjoyed. The city's determination to flout this law was a well-known frustration to those enforcement agents who took their jobs seriously.

Drinking, historically associated with many social events in New Orleans, was not easy to give up. Alcohol was consumed at Mardi Gras, on New Year's Eve, at family celebrations, at funerals, and at just about any other activity that brought together a crowd. Banning booze was akin to assaulting the city's culture. If some parishes in Louisiana elected to be dry, that was a local decision. But the federal government did not know anything about the customs of New Orleans, the city's residents contended, and many resented the one-size-fits-all prohibition against what was generally considered a right.

The Roman Catholicism of French, Spanish, and Italian inhabitants was a significant factor in the city's resistance to Prohibition. Drinking alcohol was a part of religious ritual; mass was celebrated with wine. A related reason New Orleanians overwhelmingly rejected the temperance movement was that it was driven, in their minds, by a few loud Protestants, and it merely seemed foolish. And since the local majority disdained a temperance brought on by a few, they felt validated in ignoring the Volstead Act. Even today, New Orleanians proudly tell stories passed down by relatives about the city's lack of cooperation with Prohibition laws.

Indeed, most people didn't think Prohibition would actually become law. That may help explain why the strongly pro-temperance campaign from the Protestant-led Anti-Saloon League was so vehement, vocal, and organized, while their opponents' efforts were only half-hearted and haphazard. The wet supporters in New Orleans were simply not as prepared for and organized against a movement they considered preposterous. But they were deluding themselves. There had been evidence, widely ignored by wet supporters, that the state was moving toward drier attitudes. Among those warning signs were the state's local option law of 1902, which allowed voters in individual parishes to decide whether to issue liquor licenses or to go dry. This was followed by the Gay-Shattuck Law (1909), which required bars to be three hundred feet from schools and churches, prohibited gambling in businesses serving alcohol, and imposed racial segregation on drinking establishments.

With Prohibition looming, on New Year's Eve, 1919, New Orleanians prepared by drinking champagne and other alcohol in much greater quantities than usual. In the days before the law went into effect, bars stockpiled alcohol and sales were reportedly excellent. When Prohibition began, saloons became speakeasies overnight, and they were packed with sufficient inventory to at least get them started down their criminal paths. The people of the city seemed ready and willing to become felons, too, if not in support of their principles, at least in support of their culture.

A case in point is Léon Bertrand Arnaud Cazenave, Count Arnaud, as he was affectionately known, who founded the iconic Arnaud's Restaurant about a year before Prohibition became law. Not being able to sell alcohol was a blow to his fledgling business's bottom line. So the count, born in France and unwilling to accept what seemed an absurd law, continued to sell alcohol in coffee cups in back rooms. The law eventually caught up with him, and he was arrested. Arnaud's Restaurant was closed, and the count was held in jail until his federal trial for violating the Volstead Act. But he won the jury over and was acquitted, allowing him to reopen Arnaud's before Prohibition ended. Count Arnaud's position in defense of drinking made him a local hero and bolstered his restaurant's business.

Other bars and restaurants padlocked during Prohibition included Turci's, Delmonico's, the Old Absinthe House, and Commander's Palace. But some establishments managed to sell alcohol without getting caught. Tom Anderson's Saloon, a former Storyville establishment, was known for serving liquor procured through various sources that didn't poison its customers. And close to City Park, the Holland House (formerly Lamothe's Tavern), run by Anthony Campagno and his sons, boasted fine dining upstairs and an ice cream parlor downstairs, which shielded the bar in the back. The bar was famous for gambling and for serving bartender Nick Campagno's Manhattans, reputed to be the best in town. Well-known New Orleans gambler Robert "Beansy" Fauria operated in a back room, making book and providing gambling tables. He was the Campagno family's conduit for good smuggled liquor, such as Canadian whiskey and scotch, as well as rye and other spirits that came through Honduras. Beansy also served as a protector, since he paid the local police well. The Holland House was near the racetrack, so bookmaking, drinking, and excellent eating were conveniently located for fans of the horses.

MANHATTAN
—— Makes 1 drink ——

2 ounces rye

1 ounce Italian vermouth

2 dashes Angostura bitters

A maraschino cherry or orange peel for garnish

Stir drink ingredients together with ice in a cocktail shaker and strain into a chilled cocktail glass. Garnish with a maraschino cherry or orange peel.

It's interesting to note that long before Prohibition was the law of the United States, privateers, or legalized pirates, were smuggling alcohol from New Orleans into Louisiana's dry parishes and into dry areas of other states. Prohibition-era smugglers and rumrunners were said to have used the old routes of legendary nineteenth-century privateer Jean Lafitte, which ran through Barataria Bay and the barrier islands along the Gulf of Mexico.

Liquor stores built just inside the Orleans parish line were notorious during this period, taking advantage of the rather loose enforcement of the law. When Prohibition was in force, bootleggers exhibited incredible ingenuity, using coffins, hot water bottles, and gasoline cans to smuggle alcohol. U.S. Department of Justice reports contain lively accounts of their creativity and imagination.

By making liquor available, rumrunners performed a valuable service for the city that seemed to make a point of drinking more during Prohibition. Rumrunners and moonshiners were kept so busy that a plentiful supply actually made the price of alcohol decline. And New Orleans, with its reserve of illegal booze and its key position on the Mississippi River, seized the opportunity to supply rum and other spirits to the rest of the thirsty nation.

The record clearly supports the fact that New Orleans was considered the wettest place in the country throughout Prohibition. The ease of obtaining alcohol could only take place with a uniform disregard for the law, not only from people on the street, but from state and local government.

Prohibition was in effect when Huey P. Long was elected governor of Louisiana in 1932. Long was no fan of the law, and it is said that when asked what he would do to help enforce it, he retorted, "Nothing." In their attempt to save the city from Prohibition, the city council of New Orleans tried to have alcohol declared a food, and therefore exempt from the ban.

The federal government did try to stop unlawful activity in New Orleans. It ordered coast guard boats to actively patrol the Gulf of Mexico and be prepared to sink vessels engaged in rum-running. Federal agents padlocked speakeasies in order to publicly mark them, a visible reminder of the Volstead Act. This resulted in more speakeasies shut down in New Orleans than in any other city in the United States.

During this period, the federal government was also responsible for the literal poisoning of industrial alcohol in order to discourage its use for human consumption. At first, bootleggers used chemists to remove these adulterants, but the federal government continued to add more and more toxic ingredients. It is estimated that about ten thousand people around the country died from this poisoning, enraging the citizenry. This was one way among many that Prohibition contributed to increased cynicism toward the federal government, and it made heroes of those willing to stand up against the law—often not for reasons of morality, but merely out of defiance. Another unintended result of Prohibition was the likely increase in police graft, bribery, and political corruption that accompanied its attempted enforcement.

Regardless of possible penalties, throughout the thirteen years of Prohibition, New Orleanians frequently and humorously thumbed their noses at authority. For example, the signal to customers at a speakeasy that a federal agent was in the house was for the band to play "How Dry I Am." Hearing the song meant that it was time to leave or to consume the evidence.

The often-told story of federal agent Isadore "Izzy" Einstein can be found in reports filed with the U.S. Department of Justice. Einstein's job was to determine how well Prohibition was faring around the country by seeing how long it took him to procure alcohol after arriving in a new city. In New Orleans, as the story goes, Einstein arrived at the airport and hailed a taxi to ride downtown. He asked the taxi driver—a traditional font of insider information about a city—if he knew of a place where a person could get a drink. The taxi driver reached under his seat and offered a flask to Einstein. This mere thirty-five seconds made New Orleans the hands-down winner in the "find a drink" competition.

As in other cities, Prohibition brought an increase in organized crime and social disintegration. But in New Orleans, organized crime did not grow to the extent that it did in, for example, Chicago. One likely reason was the preference of both local law enforcement and consumers for the continued operation of speakeasies and restaurants by the same entrepreneurs who had run the establishments before Prohibition. The people of New Orleans seem to have decided that amateur citizen felony was a better choice than professional crime and that there was no need for organized crime to step in and supply illegal hooch.

One reason for the demise of Prohibition was the ability of the wealthy to stockpile alcohol for private consumption. The poor were most affected and controlled by their lack of access to alcoholic beverages. That inequality began to rub the wrong way. An example of the elitism that Prohibition engendered was the Southern Yacht Club's practice of holding regular dances at its quarters by Lake Pontchartrain. There, New Orleanians who could afford the yachting—or at least the boating—life enjoyed the club's signature cocktail, the Pink Lady (or, as it was also known, the Pink Shimmy), which had a residual resemblance to the Ramos Gin Fizz without the fizz. Dances at the lakefront with drinks and jazz bands were a decidedly privileged activity. This disparity of access to alcohol was particularly poignant because of the leveling effect of regular drinking establishments, which had historically been places where the sharing of a drink, regardless of income or class, was a sign of equality and respect.

PINK LADY OR PINK SHIMMY
—— *Makes 1 drink* ——

Those fortunate enough to know a pharmacist, a physician, or someone else with legitimate access to grain alcohol—and who was willing to share it—might make gin by flavoring it with juniper oil. This gin was pretty rough. Drinks concocted during Prohibition reflect the need to make the liquor palatable, and are not remembered for their finesse on the tongue or nuances of flavor. Thus the Pink Lady was popular at a time when cream was used to mask a lot of burn from the alcohol. Armond Schroeder, a Southern Yacht Club manager, is credited with adding heavy cream to the traditional Pink Lady, which did not originally contain cream.

2 ounces gin

**1 or 2 teaspoons grenadine, depending on
how sweet you like your drink**

White of a raw egg

½ ounce heavy cream

1. Place all ingredients in a cocktail shaker with five cubes of ice. Close shaker and shake vigorously until mixture is foamy and frothy. Be sure to mix well so that cream and egg are thoroughly emulsified.

2. Strain into a chilled cocktail glass.

Although it was happily consumed by both sexes during Prohibition, the Pink Lady suffered the fate of becoming known as a female drink, perhaps in part because of the drink's color, and also because the alcohol was masked by the cream and egg. During the post–World War II era, with the increased emphasis on traditional gender roles, this girly drink went out of favor. In an often-ignored legacy of Prohibition, however, women who drank in public were there to stay. Prior to 1920, many bars and saloons were male-only establishments. During Prohibition, so many restaurants and speakeasies openly sold spirits to women that the practice carried over into post-Prohibition days. All kinds of women, not simply prostitutes and the avant garde, could drink and have fun in public establishments.

Prohibition turned out to be an expensive experiment. In addition to the cost of new agencies created to enforce the law, the government lost revenue in the form of taxes it had been collecting on alcohol.

When the country was ready to bring the great experiment to an end, statistics show that New Orleans was still the city with the most saloons serving drinks and the most padlocked places. The padlocks indicated how many establishments did not stop serving alcohol when the Volstead Act went into effect and were thus ostentatiously closed by federal agents.

During the first week after Prohibition was officially lifted on December 5, 1933, more than nine hundred beer permits were issued in the Crescent City. New Orleanians still repeat the apocryphal story that when Prohibition was repealed, church bells rang in celebration all over the city.

Arguably the most famous bar in New Orleans in the twentieth century, Pat O'Brien's began on St. Peter Street as a well-known Prohibition-era speakeasy called the Club Tipperary. By the time it opened, speakeasies had reinforced doors and required passwords; the secret words to enter the Club Tipperary were "Storm's brewing." Two days before the repeal of Prohibition went into effect, the club reopened as Pat O'Brien's just down the street from its first location. A few years later, O'Brien and his new partner, Charlie Cantrell, moved down the street again to open at its current location, 718 St. Peter.

Pat O's, as it is affectionately known, is one of the most familiar landmarks in the French Quarter. The bar has grown from its original smallish space; its famous courtyard now graces postcards sent around the world. The fountain—with flaming jets of natural gas arcing through the waters—has seen celebrity antics as well as the playful and alcohol-induced revelry of lesser-known carousers. In an earlier era, Pat O's was known for protecting the activities of the famous people who came to drink there.

Before Pat O'Brien's opened as a legal bar, its customers drank rum smuggled in from the Caribbean. When Prohibition ended, long-deprived patrons were ready for spirits such as bourbon, rye, and scotch; consequently, rum lost its popularity. But during the 1940s, American distilleries were tasked with distilling for the World War II effort, which made bourbon and other grain-based spirits hard to obtain. Scotch production was also interrupted by the war, so it, too, was in short supply. Rum once again was just about all anyone could get.

After the war, the now-coveted grain spirits needed time to get back into production and become ready for sale. In the interim, in an attempt to rid themselves of an overstock of rum, suppliers required buyers to purchase a specific number of cases of rum for each case of whiskey. That left bar owners with too many cases of unwanted rum. Pat O'Brien responded to this dilemma by creating a sweet drink made with lemon juice, passion-fruit syrup, and a double shot of rum. The powerful pink drink was named the Hurricane.

This famous French Quarter bar claims that the Hurricane was invented on its premises, and it certainly has popularized the drink. That cannot be disputed. Historians, however, have found that the Hurricane was a drink available at the 1939 World's Fair in New York. But most who drink at Pat O'Brien's do not care about the Hurricane's history. They are simply happy to be drinking a Hurricane there.

In 1978, Pat O'Brien's was purchased by George Oechsner, Jr., and his family still owns and operates the bar, which has developed many traditions. For example, two grand pianos form a platform for dueling piano performances, and song requests are submitted on napkins. The pianos are topped with copper, as are the tables and the bar itself. In addition to the Hurricane, the bar offers other storm-centric drinks, such as the Squall, the Cyclone, the Typhoon, and the Breeze. It seems that ever since the days of the speakeasy password, there has always been heavy weather developing at Pat O's. Now the bar has locations in San Antonio and Orlando, where they are ambassadors of the New Orleans attitude.

Much mythology has grown up around the Hurricane glass. One likely story is that a salesman had a quantity of shapely glasses and sold them to the bar for a good price. The glasses had a shape reminiscent of a hurricane shade—a glass shade that sits on a table to protect the candle within from the winds of the storm, and a very familiar shape in New Orleans. A name and a brand were born: this traditional undulating shape with a footed stem is the Pat O's glass. The iconic glass can be purchased as a souvenir with or without the drink inside. Many a young adult has celebrated achieving drinking age by taking home a Hurricane glass from Pat O's as a trophy.

HURRICANE

—— *Makes 1 drink* ——

This is a Hurricane in the modern vein, reminiscent of the fruity rum punch served at Pat O's today. This drink is greatly improved by using fresh juice. And the drink is sweet, so be careful with the simple syrup.

2 ounces pineapple juice

2 ounces orange juice

1 ounce white rum

1 ounce dark rum

1 ounce passion-fruit juice (maracuja)

1 ounce simple syrup (optional)

¾ ounce lime juice

Dash of bitters

Crushed ice

Cherries, pineapple, orange, and lime slices for garnish

1. Shake all drink ingredients over ice to combine well and chill.

2. Strain into a large glass filled with crushed ice. Garnish with fruit.

HURRICANE 2

—— Makes 1 drink ——

This version is closer to what the original cocktail may have been.

1 ounce white rum

1 ounce dark rum

½ ounce passion-fruit syrup

1 tablespoon lime juice

Cherries, orange slices, etc., for garnish

1. Mix drink ingredients together. Shake over ice to combine and chill.

2. Strain into a glass filled with crushed ice. Garnish with fruit.

Prohibition law did allow individuals to make fruit wine and cider, and a household could make up to two hundred gallons per year. So, many who could not afford speakeasies and who were unwilling to risk buying moonshine did make wine and cider.

Others preferred to engage in outright civil disobedience and distill their own whiskey. Some people justifiably felt that danger lurked in drinking or buying alcohol in public, and they felt safer producing their own spirits. Also, on the whole, moonshine was cheaper than bootleg spirits. Another big advantage was that home brewing gave the distiller control over the product.

It was certainly possible to buy the hardware and necessary ingredients to distill basement or backroom spirits and brews. A pot still, the traditional European means of distilling still in use today, is made of copper and has a lid or head with an attached tube. The heavy copper pot conducts heat quickly and also cools fast. The tube, known as the worm, is usually coiled and sits in a barrel or other vessel of water where it is passively cooled. The worm allows gases to condense. The material that is distilled, known as distiller's beer, is usually a mash of fermented grain, although anything that has been fermented can be distilled. The distiller's beer is placed in the pot. The head is placed on the pot and the joint is sealed. A fire under the pot heats the beer, and vapors given off rise into the cooled worm, where they condense. The liquefied vapors are collected in a cistern. In order to make the resulting spirits smoother, the liquid that has been collected can be distilled again. This can be done in a second still or in the same still after it has been cleaned. The result of this process is a clear, uncolored liquid—moonshine. Moonshine can be diluted with water to adjust its alcohol level, and it can also be flavored.

✦ DISTILLER'S BEER AND MASH ✦

Distiller's beer is made by placing grain in a mash tub, approximately a bushel to twelve gallons of water. After the grain is stirred well, the tub is filled with water and boiled. The water is cooled, and to it malt and a half bushel of a second grain are added. The mash is stirred, allowed to boil again and cooled, and yeast is then stirred in.

Sweet mash is the result of cooking the grain before adding the yeast. Sour mash is the result of using beer after the distilling process is complete to inoculate new mash. By using the sour mash method, the distiller can ensure consistency between batches. Sour mash inoculation results in a more acidic (or sour) mash, and the low pH helps keep bacterial contamination to a minimum.

Liquid heated in the still with the fermented grains is called a mash. A wort, used for making scotch, is a liquid that has the solids removed after fermentation and before it is placed in the pot of the still. The wort makes the still easier to clean.

Distilled spirits can be finished by filtering through charcoal. As an alternative to a second distillation, this filtering process can remove the fusel oils, a mixture of several alcohols other than ethanols produced as a by-product of fermentation.

During Prohibition, the often harsh quality of moonshine, which was unaged, called for flavoring. Gin could be made by adding juniper oil. Rum was approximated by adding brandy. Flavoring with herbs, fruits, and sugar was routine in order to make the moonshine palatable.

CHERRY BOUNCE

This recipe was a moonshiner's approximation of traditional cherry bounce.

1. Make a strong tea of cherry bark. It should be highly colored and smell of cherry.

2. Add tea to the spirits and add sugar syrup to taste.

TRADITIONAL CHERRY BOUNCE

—— *Makes about 2 quarts* ——

A popular eighteenth- and nineteenth-century cordial, said to be a favorite of George Washington.

1 pound fresh cherries, pitted and stemmed

4 cups brandy, rum, or other spirit of choice

2¾ cups granulated sugar

¼ of a fresh nutmeg

1-inch piece of cinnamon stick

1. Place cherries, brandy, and sugar in a gallon jar. Stir well to fully dissolve sugar and slightly bruise fruit.

2. Add nutmeg and cinnamon stick. Cover and store in a cool, dark location for 45 days. Shake jar occasionally to fully incorporate sugar.

3. After 45 days, remove cherries and spices with a slotted spoon, leaving as much liquid in jar as possible. Allow remaining liquid to settle. Either decant until solids are reached or strain through a coffee filter. Discard solids. Serve at room temperature. Refrigerate leftovers.

BATHTUB GIN

—— *Makes 1 liter* ——

During Prohibition, making gin—a flavored redistillation of neutral spirits—was preferred over whiskey, because whiskey required aging for best taste. Using grain alcohol and water and flavoring it with juniper berries and other spices was the usual recipe. Of course, during Prohibition, people often used denatured alcohol, which caused illness and death.

½ liter grain alcohol
½ liter water
Peel of one lemon
⅛ cup dried juniper berries

Place all ingredients in jar or bottle and close the lid. Keep in cool, dark place, like a closet. Shake jar each day. In about a week, strain out solids.

Other botanicals such as anise seed can also be added. A smoother flavor can be obtained by using 100-proof vodka.

RIVERBOATS AND
THE MISSISSIPPI RIVER

Sometimes too much to drink is barely enough.
—MARK TWAIN

The Mississippi River helped shape the drinking culture of New Orleans. Starting at Lake Itasca in Minnesota, the river carries the soil of thirty-one states and a bit of Canada past New Orleans. Not only is the mighty Mississippi a metaphor for life's journey, but it is also a real highway of goods, services, travelers, gamblers, ideas, and spirits.

Most early travel and trade down the Mississippi took place by flatboat or keelboat, taking advantage of the swift and dangerous current to power the journey. Large quantities of goods, including spirits, made upriver and along the eastern tributaries were thus made readily available in New Orleans. In the story of spirits, told through the ledgers of those who made it, New Orleans looms large as a marketplace. But flatboats and barges could not make the trip back up the river. Crews often walked or rode home, while the boats were usually disassembled and the lumber put to other uses. (Many a house in New Orleans is made of barge boards.) There was a cabin on flatboats that carried passengers, and the long trip was an opportunity for passengers with nothing else

94

to do to spend time drinking in the bar. Likewise, there was little for the crew to do on the lengthy journey besides drink.

The keelboat was the round-trip mode of transportation on the Mississippi. It was long and pointed at both ends to minimize resistance and create maximum maneuverability. At first the boats were small, but they grew to be about seventy-five feet long. Going downriver was easy; the river did most of the work. Going upriver was another story. To accomplish this enormous task, a crew of about twenty-five manned both sides of the boat, each plunging a long pole into the river bottom and "walking" from bow to stern, propelling the boat upstream. The crew also used ropes called cordelles, which were wrapped around tree trunks and other sturdy posts and used as pulleys to propel the boats. They also grabbed at overhanging branches (called bushwhacking) and any other available handholds. Most keelboats had sails, too, which could be counted on when the wind was right. In this manner, goods from Europe and the Caribbean made their way from New Orleans upstream at a rate of about fifteen miles per day. In both directions, the journey was treacherous. Keelboats were menaced by the current, the tendency of the riverbank to collapse, and threats from bands of thieves.

Keelboatmen, using brute force against the mighty river, were muscular and strong. They came to value fighting and feats of strength, challenging other keelboat crews to what they called "rough frolics." Keelboatmen boasted of being half alligator and half man, and fascinated others by their strength, as well as by their ability to exchange blows and dance and carouse. These men became even more ferocious when fueled by the spirits they found at the port of New Orleans.

The invention of the steamboat in the early nineteenth century transformed river travel and commerce. By the 1830s, there were over

1,200 steamboats traveling the Mississippi. As steamboats became more common, keelboatmen began to float downriver with cargo, sell their boats in New Orleans, and steam back up the river. Sometimes they steamed upriver as passengers, but more often they crewed the steamboats. Gradually, steamboats gained dominance on the river and keelboats only operated on tributaries not navigable by steamboats. As the wild keelboatmen became the crew and pilots of the steamboats, steamboats gained a reputation for rowdiness.

In addition to drinking, gambling was a way to pass the time during the long hours passengers waited to arrive at their destinations. The saloons and bars on riverboats were leased in the same manner as space on land and were outfitted by the lessee. These saloons served the drinks being consumed at bars all over the country. But because the upriver leg of the journey began in New Orleans, the liquor was stocked there, so the journey had a very New Orleans taste.

Steamboats gained dominance on the Mississippi River at the same time bourbon was rising in popularity. The steamboat carried cargoes of bourbon to New Orleans, where, in saloons and bars, bittered slings were available, as was ice to chill food and cocktails. A taste for these niceties traveled from New Orleans to points upriver.

❧ BOURBON ❧

As the United States expanded westward, rum became less popular; it was an expensive and difficult commodity to transport over mountains or over long distances. A still, however, could be easily moved and provided the means of producing liquor from whatever was locally available. The stills that operated in the late eighteenth and early nineteenth centuries were mostly farm stills. Licenses of the day show that liquor was made by farmers, who sometimes lent out or leased their stills to others who paid taxes on their production.

Bourbon becomes bourbon by the aging of corn whiskey. The distilled product was placed in oak barrels burned on the inside to the point of charring. This process was hardly a new invention. Charcoal was used by the Romans as a filtering agent. The French used it to age and flavor brandy. It was not a great leap to take another distilled product and store it in the same manner. The use of the charred-oak barrels lent a reddish color, as well as distinctive flavors, to the whiskey.

An important component of any whiskey is the quality of water used. The water in Kentucky is naturally filtered through limestone. It does not contain the off-flavored iron found in water in many other parts of the country. The aging process is enhanced by the state's hot summers, which force the spirits into the wood cells of the barrels. Conversely, the cold winters pull the spirits out of the wood. In both instances, the spirits pass through charcoal and pick up the caramel and vanilla flavors of the oak.

Where and when the name "bourbon" arose is a matter of speculation. It seems to have been in widespread use by the mid-nineteenth century. There is a Bourbon County, Kentucky. According to one story, invoices from a place called Limestone in Bourbon County accompanied a shipment of the spirit to New Orleans. New Orleanians liked what they drank, and topers in the city began to seek out spirits from Bourbon County. This story has been disputed, however, since Limestone was part of Bourbon County for only a short time. Cocktail historian Michael R. Veach speculates that it was merely a marketing ploy used after the Louisiana Purchase.

Initially, barrels of bourbon made their way to New Orleans via barge. Records show that unaged spirits were not popular in New Orleans, one of the largest markets for spirits. What the buyers in New Orleans preferred had great influence on what distillers produced. New Orleanians already had a taste for brandy, which was an aged distillate of wine. The vanilla and caramel flavors not only enriched the brandy, but removed its rough edge. Veach speculates that marketers were the ones who decided to age raw bourbon as a value-added step, since they were more in touch with the buyers' requirements and predilections.

The column still, also called the continuous still, was invented in the 1830s. Unlike the pot still, which was a simple heat-and-condense operation, the column still worked in a more complex way. It was extremely tall, sometimes up to three stories high, and was loaded continuously with brewer's beer from the top. At intervals, perforated plates with offset large holes directed the mash or brewer's beer. The spent grains were removed from the bottom through a small door. Steam introduced at the bottom of the column traveled up through the perforations and heated the beer. The heated beer released its alcohol, which was then condensed through the worm, or coil, and collected. As long as beer was being introduced into the column, alcohol was being made. The column did not require removing solids from the beer to prevent scorching before heating, and thus eliminated the need to clean the still over and over. These efficiencies increased the profit that could be had in the distilling process and made large-scale production commercially feasible.

Other innovations included a new method of regulating the temperature of the mash. If the mash gets too hot, the heat kills the yeast. When the yeast is killed, the fermentation process stops and no more alcohol is produced. Ideally, the temperature should be high enough to release alcohol vapors but low enough to keep the yeast alive.

Another important advance involved the storage of barrels. Originally, barrels were stored in the manner of cognac and brandy barrels—that is, upright, stacked about three high in a staggered formation. The trouble with this traditional method was that the weight of the upper barrels caused the bottom barrels to leak, which meant loss of product. The tight pattern that was formed also prevented air circulation, encouraging the growth of mold, which gives a musty flavor to spirits. The improvement came with the invention of a trestle system to hold the barrels on their sides. The second and third rows of barrels rested on supports, not the barrels underneath, thus eliminating the weight problem and increasing air circulation. Another benefit of the trestle system was that it allowed any barrel to be removed from storage without disturbing other barrels.

Distillers already knew that during the aging process, hot weather drove spirits into the wood of the barrels and cool weather allowed it to recede from the wood. To speed the process, distillers heated the warehouses where the barrels were stored, so that an extra aging cycle could be squeezed into a year.

During this period, rectifiers began processing bourbon. These were wholesalers who bought product from a number of distilleries, blended it, and sold it. They did not distill. They finished the product, not necessarily by aging, but by adding flavorings and colorants. Flavorings could include brown sugar, prune juice, or tea, which added sweetness and color. Some of the recipes were later pressed into service during Prohibition years to flavor and color moonshine. The rectifiers did not really make bourbon; they simply altered it. The price of their product reflected the fact that it wasn't aged bourbon.

Dr. James Crow brought a scientific method of observation and record keeping to the distilling process. He understood that temperature could not only kill yeast, but also affect the proof of the product. He therefore used a thermometer to record temperatures during the distilling process, determining the optimal temperature for best results and ensuring a consistent product. Crow has been called the father of bourbon. He introduced other innovations in production, the most significant of which was to keep the equipment and surrounding area clean and free from contaminants such as microbes, mold, and dirt. His name is memorialized in Old Crow bourbon, for many years considered the highest standard.

BOURBON SOUR

—— *Makes 1 drink* ——

1 teaspoon fine sugar

2 teaspoons freshly squeezed lemon juice

2 ounces bourbon

1. Muddle sugar and lemon juice in a cocktail shaker until sugar dissolves. Add bourbon.

2. Add ice to shaker and shake vigorously. Strain into a cocktail glass.

BOURBON HOT TODDY

—— *Makes 1 drink* ——

1 teaspoon brown sugar

3 ounces hot water

2 ounces bourbon

1. Dip a serving cup into a pan of boiling or very hot water.

2. Add sugar, hot water, and bourbon to warmed cup. Stir and serve.

Southern Comfort was a rectified liquor in an age when such drinks were unusual. It was developed in 1874 by Martin Wilkes Heron, a bartender in the French Quarter. The original recipe was made with real bourbon that contained fruit and spice flavorings, as well as coloring. Heron initially called his drink Cuffs and Buttons. At the World Cotton Exposition in New Orleans in 1885, the now-renamed Southern Comfort was called the "grand old drink of the South." In 1900, Heron's concoction took the gold medal for taste at the Paris World Exposition. This feat was duplicated at the World Exposition at St. Louis in 1904.

Fifteen years after creating his recipe, Heron moved to Memphis and registered the trademark for Southern Comfort. He sold it bottled and noted on the label "None Genuine But Mine" as a warning against competitors and their not-quite-as-good recipes. The original recipe is said to have contained bourbon, honey, vanilla bean, lemon, orange, cinnamon, clove, and cherries. The flavorings were macerated for a few days in the bourbon, then strained out before bottling. After he left Memphis and moved to St. Louis, Heron created a drink he called the St. Louis cocktail. It was marketed as a drink that was so tasty that no one would be able to resist it. Thus it came with the limit of two to a customer, since "no gentleman would ask for more."

NIGHTCLUBS,
TIKI BARS, AND RUM

✦ LOUNGES AND NIGHTCLUBS ✦

After Prohibition, the lounges and nightclubs found in larger American cities emerged as an important cultural phenomenon for gender equality. Lounges were natural descendants of the speakeasy, where patrons sat at tables and sometimes pretended to eat while drinking alcohol from coffee cups. Women and men alike went to speakeasies, and with that gender barrier broken, both sexes frequented lounges after Prohibition.

At a nightclub or lounge, socializing with drinks took on an air of respectability because patrons could sit at tables and were served by a waiter or waitress in the manner of a restaurant. Often, tables were large and could accommodate a substantial party. Lounges soon became places where friends met to enjoy one another's company or to celebrate special events in an adult setting.

In their heyday, nightclubs were often cavernous places with live music and dancing. Although food might be served, most nightclubs were after-dinner establishments for drinking and being entertained. Some lounges evolved into supper clubs, serving dinner early in the evening and becoming a nightclub with entertainment as the evening progressed. In New Orleans, music was often as central to the experience as food and alcohol.

The Grunewald, the Roosevelt, the Fairmont, and the Roosevelt Again

The Grunewald Hotel opened on Baronne Street in 1893, replacing Grunewald Hall, a performing arts center on the same site. Both were named after builder and owner Louis Grunewald, who had emigrated from Germany. A decade after opening, the hotel underwent a major expansion, adding four hundred rooms; the new part of the property opened in 1907. During the height of its popularity, the Grunewald operated a large catering division. It also boasted what supporters claimed was the first nightclub in the United States, the Cave, which had a low ceiling aptly decorated with fake stalactites and stalagmites, and a waterfall. Reflecting the folklore of Bavaria, the club also was adorned with nymphs and gnomes. The Cave offered a new kind of space for drinking and entertainment—in particular, jazz, with chorus girls dancing to music played by the house band as patrons relaxed in the convivial atmosphere. The idea of the nightclub was just beginning to take off, but the Cave's development was stymied by the advent of Prohibition, and it closed for good in 1930.

The Grunewald had a distinguished history. In 1923, the hotel was sold, remodeled, and renamed the Roosevelt Hotel after former U.S. president Theodore Roosevelt. Seymour Weiss became the hotel's principal owner in 1931, and he fostered its reputation for opulence. From 1932 until his death in 1935, former Louisiana governor Huey Long used the Roosevelt as his home base while serving in the U.S. Senate—not

The Grunewald Hotel, home of the Cave. In 1923, the hotel was sold, renovated, and renamed the Roosevelt. (Courtesy SoFAB Institute)

Two views of the Bavarian-themed Cave at the Grunewald, often described as the first nightclub in the United States. (Courtesy SoFAB Institute)

The **Roosevelt**
NEW ORLEANS
"*The Pride of the South*"

The Roosevelt Hotel, home base for Senator Huey Long and site of the legendary Blue Room. (Courtesy SoFAB Institute)

The famed Blue Room, a popular nightclub in the decades after Prohibition. (Courtesy SoFAB Institute)

Cocktail napkin from the Roosevelt, advertising the Ramos Gin Fizz. (Courtesy SoFAB Institute)

only for living quarters but also for his local offices. But Senator Long was not the hotel's only draw. In 1935 the Blue Room opened at the Roosevelt, replacing the long-gone Cave. The wildly popular nightclub served dinner and drinks, and entertainment included bands and famous singers such as Louis Armstrong, Ella Fitzgerald, Sophie Tucker, Frank Sinatra, and Tony Bennett.

Weiss owned the Roosevelt for thirty years. While it continued to be an important hotel, over the decades it declined and became a bit seedy. The Roosevelt received a much-needed facelift in 1965, when it was bought by a new group and renamed the Fairmont. The Fairmont was closed after Hurricane Katrina struck in 2005, but in 2009 the historic hotel reopened once again as the Roosevelt, after a renovation said to cost nearly $150 million.

Top of the Mart

The Top of the Mart lounge was located on the top floor of the International Trade Mart, at the foot of Poydras and Canal Streets. The 33-story building was the first structure in the world devoted to furthering world trade and a forerunner to the World Trade Center in New York. Dedicated in 1968, the International Trade Mart was designed by architect Edward Durell Stone, who also designed the Radio City Music Hall and the Kennedy Center for the Performing Arts. Stone's design demonstrated the importance of world trade to the culture and economy of New Orleans, reflecting its history as a center of world commerce from its beginnings. From the early 1970s to 2001, the Top of the Mart operated as a revolving lounge, giving patrons a 360-degree view of New Orleans. When it closed, the appropriately named 360 Lounge opened in its place. It closed in 2005.

Top of the Mart did not create new cocktails or present wonderful entertainment. By the time of its opening in the 1970s, nightclubs in New Orleans had given way to lounges because live entertainment was expensive and customer preferences were changing. In a building dedicated to commerce, this expansive lounge became a place where business could be conducted over drinks without the distraction of entertainment, or a place where couples could go for a special night out to enjoy the spectacular view. More than anything, Top of the Mart was a novelty, with its revolving lounge that took advantage of the building's height and an unobstructed vista of the city and the Mississippi River.

❧ THE TIKI PHENOMENON ❧

The tiki bar is only loosely suggestive of actual Polynesian culture and themes, but it is a wonderful window into what Americans imagined Polynesia to be. ("Tiki" refers to the stylized carved wooden and stone statues found in the Polynesian islands.) The American tiki movement mixes its metaphors, and the décor is consistently confused. And rum cocktails served with umbrellas are not a tradition of the Polynesian islands, although they might derive from a Caribbean tradition.

New Orleanians are always happy to claim that they invented, fostered, or protected anything to do with spirits. The tiki movement can be credited to New Orleans not because it started there, but because New Orleans created the environment that shaped the founder of the tropics-based fad, Donn Beach.

The first tiki bar, Don the Beachcomber, was opened in 1934 in Hollywood, California, by New Orleanian Ernest Raymond Beaumont Gantt, who later renamed and reinvented himself as Donn Beach. He had traveled to Polynesia and been impressed by the area's culture, so when he opened his place in Hollywood, he decided to incorporate Polynesian motifs. He ended up decorating his bar with a fantasy version of Polynesia: rattan, torches, and leis. Beach's wife, Cora Irene "Sunny" Sund, was also an entrepreneur. While Beach was off doing military service during World War II, she expanded their tiki bar gimmick to over ten locations. In the style of the day, the restaurants served Cantonese food, which was seen as unusual and exotic. And they specialized in rum drinks with tropical fruit juices and flavored syrup.

After the war, Beach took his concept to Hawaii and opened a restaurant there, where he continued to serve innovative cocktails. He died in 1989. His original Don the Beachcomber was frequented by many Hollywood celebrities, including Charlie Chaplin and Howard Hughes.

Not long after Don the Beachcomber opened, a second tiki restaurant, Trader Vic's, opened in Oakland, California. Trader Vic was really Victor Bergeron, and his restaurant would grow into a worldwide chain. Both northern and southern Californians embraced the tiki phenomenon in its infancy. Interestingly, the convergence of the brainchild of Donn Beach from Louisiana with the influence of trendy California are what made tiki begin to move east across America: in essence, the fun and open attitude toward drinking in New Orleans and the trendiness of all things California created the tiki movement. In the world of spirits, the tiki movement was responsible for the rise of rum as a liquor of choice in the shifting rum popularity cycle.

New Orleans was not to be left out of the enthusiasm for all things tiki. In 1939, the Batt family opened an amusement park on Lake Pontchartrain. Located in a part of old Milneburg, Pontchartrain Beach flourished where today the University of New Orleans's Research and

It is our endeavor to bring you the color, romance, legendary hospitality and tempting delicacies of the exotic Polynesian Islands.

Whether you be a Malihini (newcomer) or Kamaina (old-timer) to this delightful way of culinary life we are confident that you will find it a unique, delicious experience.

Bali Ha'i

at the beach

OVERLOOKING BEAUTIFUL PONTCHARTRAIN BEACH

NEW ORLEANS, LOUISIANA

Menu from the Bali Ha'i, the popular Polynesian-style restaurant at Pontchartrain Beach. (Courtesy SoFAB Institute)

TAHITIAN BREEZE .95
(During feast time South Seas Maidens find this punch refreshing)
A deft blend of two light rums with sacred fruit juice. The flavor is completed with a touch of Louisiana Cane Juice.

NATIVE DIVER .95
(As daring as its name)
The pale milk of the coconut strengthened with a blend of light and dark Jamaican rum. Rare spices and a touch of ripe Mexican lime juice complete the creation.

BALI-BALI 1.00
(The nectar of the Polynesian Gods)
The lightest of the Jamaican rums is gently combined with the finest Virgin Island rum in a chilled container. Carefully measured portions of herbs, and the aroma of Hawaiian juices, are added to complete this masterpiece in mixology.

WAIKIKI GOLD 1.00
(The delight of Hollywood's leading ladies)
Smoothly blended aged Jamaican and Haitian rums, spiced with rare herbs, and balanced by lime juice and orange honey. A delicate glass of golden nectar.

HAWAIIAN COOLER 1.25
(Originated beneath the cool swaying palms on Waikiki beach)
Delightfully chilled rums carefully poured over icy tropical juices. Exotic herbs heighten the flavor. A cooling adventure in drinking.

BORA-BORA 1.25
(As delightful as the island for which it is named)
On the sands of the sun-kissed isle Bora-Bora the natives gather in the evening to concoct and enjoy this rum-based drink which their ancestors originated centuries ago.

SOUTH PACIFIC PUNCH 1.00
(Recalls the breezy atolls, and the soft breaking of the surf)
Aged Jamaica rum tempered with ripe lime juice. A mild drink typical of South Sea Island days.

TIKI BOWL 2.00
(The epitome of all island drinks)
You will thrill to this innovation in drinking, as you sip delicate bouquets of rum from the unique Tiki Bowl. Thoughts of Island rituals come to mind as the rich aroma of this exotic drink is savored.

NAVY GROG 1.50
(Limit of two to a customer)
A flotilla of Cuban, Puerto Rican and Demerara rums, mingle on a Bay of Pontchartrain sugar cane juice. Primed for action with the juice of a lime and the chill of ice. Will assure a sweetheart to every deck.

FOGG CUTTER 1.50
(Uncrowned king of the exotic drinks)
Carefully measured portions of choice rum form the body as dashes of lemon juice, orgeat and orange honey combine to form a purely different flavor. Sipped slowly it has no equal among Polynesian drinks.

DIAMOND HEAD DAIQUIRI	.95
COBRA'S TOOTH	1.00
PADRE'S PITFALL	1.00
IMPATIENT VIRGIN	1.00
ZOMBIE	1.50
MAI TAI	1.50

GENERAL PATTON'S TANK	1.50
DR. FONG	1.50
SAMOAN TYPHOON (limit of 2)	2.00
PAGO PAGO # 1	1.50
PAGO PAGO # 2	1.00
PINA PEPE	1.75

Also your favorite American beverage

Some of the drinks offered on the Bali Ha'i menu were the Fogg Cutter and the Tiki Bowl. [Courtesy SoFAB Institute]

Technology Park stands. The beach was artificially built, with loads of sand deposited at the lake's edge to encourage bathing in the water. A midway featured various rides as well as arcade games, such as the ring toss and air rifles blowing over wooden-duck cutouts in exchange for stuffed animal prizes. And one of the amenities at Pontchartrain Beach was the Bali Ha'i, a Polynesian-style restaurant that opened in 1952, in the full blossoming of the first tiki period.

The Bali Ha'i was decorated as a fantasy of everything that could possibly be associated with Polynesia: rattan, palm fronds, netting, seashells, turtle shells, and stuffed fish. Its drinks—well-made, subtle rum concoctions—were served both in traditional tiki glasses and in coconut shells with little paper umbrellas.

The Bali Ha'i served the Cantonese-style food of the era, as well as steaks. After more than thirty years in operation, it was destroyed in a fire in 1986. There was no reopening what had become a beloved relic. The Bali Ha'i still evokes waves of nostalgia among many in New Orleans. When the restaurant was in business, the drinking age in the city was eighteen. It was too upscale for a bathing suit, but not so fancy that children were out of place. The Bali Ha'i was a fun, crazy destination where high school seniors might come for a romantic dinner and share a Tiki Bowl with two straws before walking barefoot on the beach. The Bali Ha'i served nonalcoholic versions of its punchlike libations, but even they could be served with liquor-soaked slices of citrus that flamed dramatically at the table.

ZOMBIE

—— Makes 1 drink ——

1½ ounces golden rum

1 ounce dark rum

½ ounce white rum

1 ounce lime juice

1 teaspoon pineapple juice

1 teaspoon papaya juice

1 teaspoon superfine sugar

½ ounce 151-proof rum

1. Place all ingredients except for 151-proof rum in a shaker or pitcher and stir.

2. Fill a Tom Collins glass three-quarters full with cracked ice. Pour mixture over ice.

3. Top with 151-proof rum.

FOGG CUTTER
—— *Makes 4 or more drinks* ——

8 ounces orange juice

6 ounces lime juice

6 ounces simple syrup

4 ounces light rum

4 ounces dark rum

4 ounces brandy

4 ounces gin

¼ ounce almond extract

Combine all ingredients in a pitcher. Serve in tiki glasses or tall glasses filled with ice.

MAI TAI
—— *Makes 1 drink* ——

This is the epitome of the tiki drink.

2 ounces dark rum

1 ounce lime juice

1 ounce orgeat syrup

½ ounce curaçao

1 drop vanilla extract

Lime and mint for garnish

1. Mix all drink ingredients in a cocktail shaker with ice.

2. Shake well and pour entire contents into a tall Collins glass or a tall tiki glass. Garnish with lime and mint.

Today, in the new age of tiki, bars in New Orleans are taking the tiki gods seriously. One such bar is Tiki Tolteca, located on North Peters Street above Felipe's Taqueria. Tiki Tolteca serves traditional tiki cocktails made with rum. It also offers Latin American liquors such as pisco, and it is an interesting expansion of tiki without the Cantonese food.

Because of alcohol traditions and the appreciation locals have for drink, New Orleans has drawn many cocktail, spirits, and drink experts to make the city their home. One such transplant is tiki expert Jeff "Beachbum" Berry, who has written a number of books about the tiki phenomenon. He is also a collector of tiki memorabilia and a consultant to those aspiring to open bars with an authentic tiki experience. His tiki bar, Latitude 29, is in the Bienville House Hotel in the French Quarter.

HERE IS A RECIPE FROM BEACHBUM BERRY

LUAU DAIQUIRI

—— *Makes 1 drink* ——

2 ounces white Virgin Islands rum

¾ ounce fresh lime juice

¾ ounce orange juice

½ ounce vanilla syrup

A tiare blossom, or other unscented white flower, for garnish

Shake all ingredients well with plenty of ice cubes. Strain into a chilled cocktail glass. Garnish with tiare blossom.

Rum historian Wayne Curtis also moved to New Orleans. Many other noted writers and bartenders make regular pilgrimages to the city. This community of drink experts adds enormously to the city's continuing cocktail culture.

❖ NEW RUM DISTILLERIES ❖
IN LOUISIANA

Although Louisiana is historically a sugar-producing state, rum, which is distilled from sugarcane, has been mostly produced on Caribbean islands. But in recent years, that has changed.

Celebration Distillation, formerly known as the Old New Orleans Rum Distillers, opened in the Ninth Ward neighborhood in the 1990s in an old cotton warehouse. This premium rum distillery was the brainchild of James Michalopoulos, a noted artist based in the city, and was put together by Michalopoulos and a group of musician friends. They were not experienced distillers, and the distillery is known for its unusually configured equipment. The company uses cane grown in Louisiana, and the center of production is the column still, which purifies the alcohol to over 180 proof. The distillery's first product, Old New Orleans Crystal Rum, went on sale in 1999. The company went on to produce white, spiced, and an aged rum.

The distillery flooded in the aftermath of Hurricane Katrina, ruining much of its equipment. But many barrels the flood swept out of the building were recovered floating on the floodwaters. Those early iterations of the rum from Celebration Distillation can be purchased today as the distillery's aged ten-year-old unfiltered rum. In restarting the business, Michalopoulos and his partners improved and reconfigured the distillery. They are again producing an award-winning product, using the original column still. And the company continues to use Louisiana-grown sugarcane.

Another Louisiana distillery was opened by Trey Litel and is operated by Louisiana Spirits. According to corporate legend, the company was dreamed up in a typical Louisiana setting—a duck blind in the marsh one chilly morning. The owners of Bayou Rum—avid sportsmen and Louisiana natives—were discussing the state's abundant natural resources and rich culture. "Why doesn't Louisiana have a world-class rum?" they wondered, and Bayou Rum was born. The company began building its distillery in 2011 and put Bayou Rum on the market in 2013. The distillery is located in Lacassine, in the southwestern marshes close to sugarcane fields.

Both of these modern distilleries are committed to using Louisiana sugar in their rum. They are serious about their products, but they both tell a fun story about their origins, which is emblematic of New Orleans and New Orleans drinking. Take the taste seriously, but not yourself.

CANE SQUEEZE

—— Makes 1 drink ——

This drink was created by Elizabeth Pearce, owner of Drink & Learn, a business dedicated to telling the story of New Orleans, the South, and the United States through iconic beverages. Where else but in New Orleans would such a business based on our spirited history exist? Pearce is also coauthor of *The French Quarter Drinking Companion,* a narrative guide to bars of the French Quarter, and the author of the drinking culture blog *Open Tab.* [Her original drink uses tafia, a cheap, unaged rum that might be hard to find.]

3 ounces tafia or New Orleans Crystal Rum

3 ounces water

1 ounce fresh lime juice

½ ounce Domaine de Canton ginger liqueur

1 generous spoonful cane syrup

Nutmeg for sprinkling

Mix all drink ingredients together. Serve over ice and grate nutmeg on top.

GATOR BITE™

—— *Makes 1 drink* ——

This drink was featured at the Bayou Rum inaugural toast event in 2013. It was created for Bayou Rum by award-winning mixologist Kelly Bistok of L'Auberge Lake Charles. It is easy to make with common bar ingredients. Just mix them all in a cocktail shaker and pour over ice in a tall Hurricane glass. Careful with this one, you might get bit!

¾ **ounce Bayou Rum Silver**

¾ **ounce Bayou Rum Spiced**

¾ **ounce Bayou Satsuma Rum Liqueur**

1¼ **ounces orange juice**

1¼ **ounces pineapple juice**

Splash of simple syrup

Squeeze of 3 lime wedges

Dash of grenadine

Maraschino cherry for garnish (optional)

1. Place all drink ingredients in a chilled cocktail shaker over crushed ice. Shake well to combine.

2. Pour mixture with ice into a Hurricane glass or other tall glass. Garnish with cherry.

RUM SLING

—— Makes 1 drink ——

Rum continues to be generally popular, only suffering the ebb and flow of trends. Originally, the sling was often a rum drink made with water, sugar, and sometimes citrus juice. It was supposed to be a refreshing drink and thus was usually served cool.

1 cube or teaspoon sugar

1 ounce water

2 ounces rum

Nutmeg for garnish

1. Muddle sugar and water in a tall rocks glass until sugar is dissolved. Add rum.

2. Add ice and stir. Garnish with freshly grated nutmeg.

THE MODERN
CONSEQUENCES

AFTER PROHIBITION

America has only three cities: New York, San Francisco,
and New Orleans. Everywhere else is Cleveland.

—TENNESSEE WILLIAMS

After the repeal of Prohibition, a three-tiered system of alcohol distribution was instituted throughout the United States, largely in response to the abusive control that alcohol producers had exercised over bars prior to the Volstead Act. The system was intended to prevent direct sales of alcohol from producers to consumers, and also from producers to retail sellers, such as package liquor vendors and saloons. The middle tier of the new system, between producers of alcohol and drinking or other retail establishments, was comprised of liquor distributors.

Before Prohibition, spirits producers frequently advanced money to would-be bar owners so they would have the capital to open, requiring in return that a bar buy exclusively from the original investor. Effectively, this gave liquor companies a stranglehold on bars and, in the eyes of many bar owners, excessive control over the entire liquor chain. The three-tiered system, placing distributors as buffers between producers and sellers, was designed to thwart a possible return to the restraining pre-Prohibition practices. Under the revocation amendment, states were also allowed to determine their own mechanisms for sales of package liquor and to set the legal drinking age.

The variety of state systems in existence today reflects the attitudes prevailing in those states in the 1930s. Some states created Alcoholic Beverage Control (ABC) stores. These package liquor stores were owned by the state, which set prices and made choices as to what could be bought, sold, and drunk by limiting stock. In other states, a limited number of ABC stores were licensed to sell alcohol at set prices and with a state-approved inventory. The ABC system also regulated the number of business days and store hours.

Adoption of the ABC store model reflected a suspicion of the liquor industry and a desire to maintain control over both industry and consumer. Other states have permutations of this system, either making a distinction between wine and beer and spirits, or licensing sales more broadly while maintaining control of prices and selection of spirits.

Louisiana did not adopt this system. In New Orleans, liquor can be bought in any location that has a package liquor license. This means that spirits, wine, and beer can be found in grocery stores, in many drugstores, in liquor stores, in convenience stores, and even in gas stations. New Orleanians grow up seeing that liquor is easily purchased; they also learn that alcohol is not taboo. A fifth of bourbon can join satsumas and king cake in the grocery cart. A pint of gin can sit with shampoo, toothpaste, and cold medicine in a bag from the drugstore. Although at one time there were limits on Sunday sales of alcohol, those restrictions no longer exist. Today, as long as a store is open, it can sell spirits along with its other wares.

The lack of ABC stores in Louisiana not only fosters a relaxed attitude toward alcohol and an acceptance of a place for alcohol in people's lives, but also means that the private sector selects the alcohol that will be offered for sale. As a result, a wide variety of alcohol is available to everyone, and it is chosen by many different people. And because each store is independent, competitive pricing is the norm. Liquor sales in New Orleans thus present a stark contrast to sales in more tightly controlled states, such as its neighbor to the east, Mississippi. Many people from Mississippi towns along the Gulf of Mexico come to the Crescent City on buying forays, reinforcing its reputation as a center for and source of liquor.

NAUGHTINESS AND DRINKING

New Orleans has long been known not only for drinking but also for sexual naughtiness, as exemplified today in Bourbon Street. Named for the French royal house of Bourbon, not the corn spirit, Bourbon Street was not always lined with bars.

In the late 1800s, around the time that Storyville became the New Orleans vice district, neighboring Bourbon Street boasted a mix of restaurants and personal residences. Lafcadio Hearn, a chronicler of New Orleans life, lived on Bourbon Street in the 1880s. Galatoire's Restaurant opened on "the street" in 1905. After Storyville closed, many Bourbon Street residences were converted into clubs and bars featuring comics and musicians, as well as striptease and exotic dancing. The end of the vice district meant that the marketplace could decide where vice could be plied, and by the 1940s and into the 1950s, fifty strip clubs were using sex to sell liquor on Bourbon Street.

The streetcar that ran down Bourbon Street was replaced by a bus around 1948, changing the dynamics of the street and considerably diminishing its romance. Moreover, the city allowed marketers to emphasize Bourbon Street's aspect of promiscuity, which sold vast quantities of alcohol and supported sexual tourism. Soon, out-of-towners and New Orleanians alike poured onto the street to visit its exotic establishments. Politicians like Earl Long, who favored particular and famous strippers, were prominent denizens.

Today, Chris Owens and her revue may be all that is left of the old nature of the street. But in its heyday, swanky music and dance clubs such as the 500 Club, Casino Royale, and the Show Bar were all the rage. Burlesque was reaching for art back then, and the dancing was erotic, not pornographic. Performances had themes, costumes, live music, and special effects. Dancers were imaginative and considered talented stars. Many, such as Evangeline the Oyster Girl, the Cat Girl (Lilly Christine), and Blaze Starr, were well-known. The Cat Girl, in particular, was featured on the covers of national magazines and was hailed as a New Orleans celebrity.

Beyond Bourbon Street's classy burlesque houses, however, prostitution and procurement were hard at work. And as America in general became more tolerant of public sexuality during the free-love 1960s, the street began to look tame. In order to continue to attract tourism, strippers became more naked and bolder. Go-go dancers and pole dancers became common, no longer reflecting New Orleans and its culture, but regular tawdry USA. Eventually, what could be found on Bourbon Street could be found almost anywhere, and the once-famous burlesque strip started attracting its tourists primarily with big drinks and a quick drunk. Without discriminating drinkers, the drinks themselves suffered.

Clarinetist Pete Fountain's club, the French Quarter Inn, located at 800 Bourbon Street. The inn served lounge cocktails while Fountain and his band played, 1960–70s. [Courtesy SoFAB Institute]

Before the descent into modern sexual mores and the adoption of drink mixes, the imbibers of New Orleans enjoyed a good cocktail, as can be seen in the story of Owen Brennan and the Brennan family. In 1943, Owen purchased the Old Absinthe House from Arnaud Cazenave, who goaded him by saying that the Irish couldn't run a good restaurant because they didn't know anything about food. Owen rose to the challenge, opening his Vieux Carré Restaurant on Bourbon Street in 1946. Almost a decade later, a lease dispute led him to move the restaurant to Royal Street, and he died of a massive heart attack before the renamed Brennan's Restaurant opened in 1956. Not missing a beat, Brennan's chef, Paul Blangé, and Owen's sister, Ella, developed the new Brennan's menu. And Ella's concept of the Eye Opener—a morning cocktail—coupled with the marketing of breakfast at Brennan's was a dynamite combination. This restaurant understood that the people of New Orleans thoroughly enjoyed mixed drinks. And the concept of a morning cocktail was also a nod to the traditional idea of the healthful quality of cocktails, as reflected in, for example, the early nineteenth-century practice of enjoying a morning mint julep in Virginia. Throughout the United States, cocktails were, after all, historically made to cure what made you sick the night before, and the ingredients used, including spirits, were often considered medicine. It is only America's modern Puritanism that imposes the rule of no alcohol during the day.

According to Miss Ella, during the 1940s, well-dressed diners out on the town might start out at the Old Absinthe House for a drink, then meander to a restaurant. After their meal, they often returned to the Old Absinthe House or went to another bar for a brandy or liqueur or a liqueur-based drink. World War II–era soldiers stationed in the city were naturally drawn to Bourbon Street, and Miss Ella remembers that the Stinger was a popular drink of the time, especially with navy pilots. And she tells the wonderful story of the ladies' room in the Old Absinthe House. During World War II's nightly blackouts, the Brennans, often accompanied by friends such as Count Arnaud from across the street, would drink together in the well-appointed lounge that was part of the ladies' room. Aside from being comfortable, the lounge had no windows, so they could keep the lights on without fear of violating the blackout. The revelry and enjoyment of life could not be thwarted by a war, especially when a well-fitted ladies' room was available. That is how important proper drinking was, and is, in New Orleans.

STINGER

—— *Makes 1 drink* ——

2¼ ounces brandy

**¾ ounce white crème de menthe (or less
if you do not want a sweet drink)**

Shake ingredients together with crushed ice. Strain into a
chilled cocktail glass.

BRANDY ALEXANDER

—— *Makes 1 drink* ——

Miss Ella recalls that after a meal at a French Quarter restaurant, many a person enjoyed a Brandy Alexander at the Old
Absinthe House. The cream-based drink is one of the few drinks
of this type that survived the Prohibition era. This drink, which
is almost a dessert, was improved by using brandy instead of
whatever was available, as was popular during Prohibition.

3 ounces half-and-half

1 ounce brandy

Freshly grated nutmeg for garnish

1. Place half-and-half and brandy in a cocktail shaker filled with
   ice. Shake vigorously to mix and chill the drink.

2. Strain into a large brandy snifter and garnish with nutmeg.

Like the rest of the United States, New Orleans succumbed to drink mixes. In the post–World War II era—the time of Tang—the quicker pace of modern life and the embrace of technology meant that powdered drink mixes and bottled mixes were a welcome convenience, as was frozen food in the kitchen. The lure of the shortcut was strong and made many a bar embrace the Collins mix or the sour mix that used stable ascorbic acid instead of lemon juice. Some New Orleans businesses even bottled premixed cocktails, which were basically just bottled batched drinks. At one time, for example, the Sazerac Company sold the drink ready-made, ensuring that each Sazerac served at home would taste the same. Consumers didn't have to know how to make the drink; they only had to pour. Even bartenders did not need to know how to make a Sazerac; they could simply open the bottle and pour. On Bourbon Street, where tourists were not likely to be return customers, the quick, easy practice of using bottled drinks was especially commonplace.

Batched bottled drinks could be good and consistent. A Sazerac—containing rye, an anise-flavored liquor, a bit of sugar, and bitters—might have been tastier than a powdered Collins mix. But regardless of ingredient quality, home bartenders were ready to use both powdered and bottled mixes, just as home cooks used powdered cheese in a macaroni-and-cheese mix or dehydrated mashed potatoes. This acceptance of prepackaged bar mixes coincided with the rise of the home bar. Although the bar cart and sterling silver cocktail shaker might have been found in smart homes as early as the mid-1930s, by the 1950s, when mixes became ubiquitous, drinking at home had become a part of America's cultural practice. Mixes made an instant success of home cocktails: just follow the recipe on the label. Some people went so far as to build a little bar in the corner of the new room called the den.

In a public bar, mixes meant that there was no spoilage of citrus or other fruit. Indeed, mixes eliminated the need for fruit juice at all, thereby making bartender prep very limited. Taking on a less important role in the cocktail-making process, the bartender just selected the right bottles and poured over ice. This tendency of professional bartenders toward bottled and powdered mixes began the decline of the fine art of the cocktail. And across the United States, a generation who grew up with the taste of premixed cocktails began to eschew the cocktail altogether in favor of ever-improving American wines. Just as rye and, later, bourbon, became American spirits, American wines became the new drinks of choice.

Mr. B's Bistro, another Brennan-family restaurant, opened in 1979, after wine drinking became popular. This was the time when American wines were winning international blind taste tests, when several California wines equaled French and other European wines in quality. Mr. B's wanted to be recognized for its excellent domestic wine list. Since the use of prepackaged mixes had caused many cocktails to become ho-hum, being recognized for an all-American wine list was a way to tell the public that a restaurant still cared about the taste and quality of alcohol it served. This trend made sense, especially in a city with a tradition of drinking wine.

Of course, New Orleanians did not need to choose between cocktails and wine. The option of a glass of wine instead of a cocktail before or after dinner merely expanded the diner's choices. And cocktail drinking certainly did not disappear in New Orleans. As a matter of fact, Mr. B's Bistro started refocusing on cocktails around 1997. Today, many of the city's restaurants are capturing business from bars by serving well-crafted cocktails at the table, as well as excellent wines and food.

The massive numbers of Hurricanes sold today, while sweet and thirst quenching, are made with a premixed syrup and rum, and they come out identically every time. They're the pink drink in a plastic glass many people sip while walking down Bourbon Street, and most times, the drinker will be carrying a bag that contains their real Hurricane souvenir glass. In addition to Hurricane mix, Pat O'Brien's Bar, the originator of the drink, also sells bottled mixes for a Cyclone, a piña colada, a margarita, and a strawberry daiquiri, as well as a Bloody Mary mix, a sweet and sour mix, and simple syrup.

Stores, too, sell powdered and bottled versions of the Hurricane for home use. The mix will reproduce the taste experience of a Hurricane bought at Pat O'Brien's, although the atmosphere in your home may be lacking.

Another signature drink of walkers strolling up and down Bourbon Street is the Hand Grenade. This drink comes from a bar called Tropical Isle, and it is advertised as "New Orleans' most powerful drink." The Hand Grenade is legally trademarked, and Tropical Isle's owners vigilantly protect it from copycats. It is easily recognized because it is served in a tall neon green plastic vessel with a flared top and a base shaped like a hand grenade. Tropical Isle sells Hand Grenade mix in liter bottles, as well as a sugar-free version called the Skinny Hand Grenade. Also available are mixes called the Tropical Itch and the Horny Gator.

Both Pat O'Brien's and Tropical Isle sell their mixes not only in gift shops at their bars, but also on the internet, so an accurate experience of their drinks can be had without setting foot in New Orleans. These two establishments also sell party packs that include glasses and specialty cups to reproduce the party at home. For even more atmosphere, the Pat O'Brien's pack includes Mardi Gras beads, napkins, and green plastic derby hats.

For both of these companies, the experience of New Orleans is the new Bourbon Street. Bourbon Street is now known for its excesses of public drinking, loud music, and permanent Mardi Gras atmosphere. The street is largely closed to automobile traffic at night. And for the most part, the pedestrian mall—catering to tourists who want the license to drink publicly, intentionally get drunk, and feel liberated by the idea of being able to act in this way—has its place on the spectrum of New Orleans tolerance.

⟡ THE THREE-MARTINI LUNCH ⟡

In post–World War II America, business was conducted with liquor and food. Eating out with a customer was considered an appropriate business expense, and often that meal included alcohol. For years, tax laws allowed evening or midday meals that had a genuine business purpose to be deducted from profits as a legitimate expense. This practice changed for a number of reasons. Many Americans believed that only people on business expense accounts and the wealthy were able to afford an expensive meal with alcohol, and there was a class backlash against tax deductions subsidizing the luxuries of the rich or of big business. Additionally, Americans increasingly disapprove of heavy drinking as a part of business, especially if it interferes with one's ability to continue work after the meal.

During his 1976 presidential campaign, Jimmy Carter vilified the practice of allowing a business tax deduction for drinks and lunch as an improper and unfair subsidy for the rich. He promised the working classes that, if elected, he could rectify this problem. Then–vice president Gerald Ford, who was defeated by Carter, defended the practice. He said in a speech before the National Restaurant Association in 1978, "The three-martini lunch is the epitome of American efficiency. Where else can you get an earful, a bellyful, and a snootful at the same time?"

Regardless of tax laws, New Orleans was and still is a city where doing business over a meal is part of the culture. While changes in the tax code restricting the amount of a meal that can be deducted and eliminating the alcohol deduction doubtless affected the extent of eating and drinking for business, they have by no means eliminated the local practice. Getting to know a person over a meal and a drink and observing their habits are ways to cement business relationships. Interestingly, around the year 1875, bars were serving lunch for free to attract drinkers. Today, many restaurants offer almost-free martinis to attract diners.

VERY DRY MARTINI

—— Makes 2 drinks ——

Use good spirits since there is nothing to mask the flavor.

1 ounce dry vermouth

4 ounces gin

Olives for garnish

1. Place vermouth in a cocktail shaker filled with ice. Stir well and strain, discarding vermouth and retaining ice in shaker.

2. Add gin to the same ice-filled shaker. Stir again and strain into two chilled cocktail glasses. An olive is the traditional garnish.

   A bit of olive juice makes this a dirty martini. An onion garnish makes this a Gibson.

In 1987, New Orleans, with the rest of Louisiana, finally succumbed to the pressure of the federal government to raise the drinking age from eighteen to twenty-one. This did not happen without resistance. In the European fashion, drinking wine was a regular practice at the table, and thus children learned to drink wine at an early age. Drinking spirits was a more adult practice, but the threshold was traditionally low. For all alcohol, the age for drinking was regulated by parental authority, not by the civil authorities.

Children first drank wine diluted at the table with family meals. As they got older, their drinks were less and less diluted, and by the age of fifteen or so, they were drinking full-strength wine. Beer was also introduced early. All of this meant that by the late teens, a young person had likely learned how to drink alcohol. And drinking to excess was ritualized. For example, wakes were occasions when public drinking to excess was allowed, always within the protected space of the home where the wake was held, and where mourners needed to drown their grief. Joyous drinking to excess at a wedding was also permitted. Aside from culturally approved exceptions, however, drinking to excess was not sanctioned.

Even after Prohibition, when a more puritan attitude prevailed throughout the United States, youthful drinking resumed in New Orleans. The drinking age was established at eighteen in Louisiana even when the age of majority was still twenty-one. The liberal attitude about indoctrinating youth into drinking reflected the overall cultural acceptance of drinking as a part of living.

When Louisiana's drinking age was eighteen, college students and other young people would come to New Orleans to partake of the open and inviting sexual exhibitions on Bourbon Street, while flitting from place to place with a Hurricane or Hand Grenade in hand. Most often, they came from states where the drinking age was twenty-one. But although they dared to drink here, they usually had no experience drinking. This often led to drinking to excess, adding to Bourbon Street's already raucous reputation.

Children in New Orleans are often around people who drink frequently. They grow up seeing the adults around them drink with pleasure but also with responsibility. As late as the 1950s and 1960s, children were told to sip their Shirley Temple and Roy Rogers cocktails. With these nonalcoholic drinks, youngsters learned how to participate in the rituals of eating out and drinking with others. Bartenders all knew what these drinks were, and children's cocktails appeared on menus, because parents took their children out to eat, and children wanted to emulate their parents. The fact that no alcohol graced the children's cocktails was irrelevant. They were being instructed in the appropriate way to drink—that is, sipping.

Even public school fundraising fairs held on New Orleans school grounds are likely to have a beer concession. To comply with regulations that prohibit consumption of alcohol on site, the concession may be located on the sidewalk or street at one of the gates leading from the school grounds, but it will be visible and visited during the fair. Children know that their parents are stepping out to have a beer, and it is not a scandal. No one drinks to excess. It is just a way of increasing the enjoyment of the public activity. The sale of alcohol also increases the coffers of the school fair.

Until the legal drinking age was raised, teens who were too old for a pretend cocktail but under eighteen could have wine in restaurants when their parents allowed it. The practice was very simple. A teen with parents at a restaurant would have his place at the table set with a wine glass. If wine was ordered, when the waiter came to the table he would look at the parent/host. He would hesitate with the bottle over the glass that belonged to the teen. With a nod from the parent, the waiter would pour into the glass. This, too, did not cause a scandal. It was considered an important way for teens to transition into adulthood. Wine was food. The protocol of drinking was something learned under watchful supervision. It was a privilege of budding adulthood and became a way to welcome teens into maturity. This practice was in full force in the 1960s when Liz Williams remembers being served wine in restaurants all over the city while eating out with the family.

New Orleans was long protective of what it considered the very civilized practice of teaching the young to drink. Although no one could vote at the age of eighteen until the Twenty-Sixth Amendment was adopted in 1971, people in Louisiana could drink at the age of eighteen. Some states reduced the drinking age to eighteen upon the passage of the amendment, reasoning that if the age of majority marked the age when voting and draft eligibility were permitted, drinking should be allowed as well. This prompted a group known as Mothers against Drunk Driving (MADD) to begin a campaign to return the drinking age to twenty-one, asserting that highway deaths and accidents caused by drinking could be reduced by raising the drinking age. Based on the recommendations of the Presidential Commission on Drunk Driving, Congress enacted the Uniform Drinking Age Act, which was signed into law by President Ronald Reagan on July 17, 1984. That law gave states five years to raise the drinking age to twenty-one, or to lose millions of dollars available to the states as federal highway funds.

Louisiana finally succumbed to the threat of losing federal highway funds and raised the drinking age; it was among the last ten states to do so. Louisiana law, however, still allows parents to permit a child to drink. Children are also allowed to drink alcohol for medical purposes. The exceptions are spelled out in Louisiana Revised Statutes 14:93.10.

When the law was first passed, it complied with the letter of the requirements of the Uniform Drinking Age Act. The Louisiana law made it illegal for a person under the age of twenty-one to buy alcohol. It did not make it illegal for a person to sell alcohol to a minor. In 1995, the state finally made it illegal to sell alcohol to those under the legal drinking age. MADD argues that the minimum drinking age of twenty-one has reduced alcohol-related driving accidents and deaths. Others argue that it causes drinking to go underground and encourages binge drinking. In Louisiana, there is a general belief that our way—teaching people to drink by recognizing it in a larger cultural context—is not a bad way to learn how to enjoy alcohol.

SHIRLEY TEMPLE

—— Makes 1 drink ——

4 ounces ginger ale

2 teaspoons grenadine syrup

Maraschino cherry for garnish

Stir together ginger ale and grenadine over ice in an old-fashioned glass. Garnish with maraschino cherry.

ROY ROGERS

—— Makes 1 drink ——

4 ounces cola

2 teaspoons grenadine syrup

Maraschino cherry for garnish

Stir together cola and grenadine over ice in an old-fashioned glass. Garnish with maraschino cherry.

❧ THE OPEN CONTAINER LAW ❧

In New Orleans, it is legal to walk outside while holding an open container of alcohol. This is why drinkers on Bourbon Street can meander up and down the street carrying a plastic cup of their favorite beverage, stopping at takeout windows for refills. Patrons of restaurants or bars can also take a cup to go, known locally as a go-cup, instead of chugging what is left in a glass before leaving.

At one time, restaurants with drive-through windows would sell drinks to go. A driver could buy a drink (served in a glass or plastic cup) and drive away with it, or drink it in the car in the parking lot. In 2004, the law was changed to prohibit drivers from having open containers, although passengers could have an open alcoholic beverage. That made it possible for a driver to pass his drink to a passenger if he was stopped by the police. Later, the law was changed to prohibit all open containers in cars. Now the old restaurant drive-through windows selling drinks are gone as well. Drive-through daiquiri stands still exist, but since 2004 they can only sell daiquiris in sealed containers.

The ability to have open containers outdoors is an important element of the drinking culture of the city. Not only does it attract the tourist out for a massive public drunk, but the law also facilitates other cultural practices, such as Mardi Gras, when drinking in the street is almost mandatory. During Carnival, members of walking clubs parade around town pulling rolling coolers full of beer and other alcoholic drinks. Parade watchers carry picnic fare and alcoholic beverages to enjoy with their meal as they watch the bands and floats go by. Public drinking also means that picnics in the park or on the seawall of Lake Pontchartrain can include wine, beer, and cocktails. And drinking during festivals and other public events is not only allowed, but expected. St. Patrick's Day, St. Joseph's Day, Halloween, Southern Decadence, and public tailgating for sports events all include public drinking, and the laws that allow it are a reflection of the cultural belief that drinking is a communal activity that people should share, both elegantly and profanely, as part of the celebration of living.

In August 2013, a petition appeared online to protect the New Orleans go-cup from a new threat. The villain was an anti-litter campaign, and as new bars opened in areas close to residential neighborhoods, they were being restricted from giving out go-cups. This was not a reaction to public drinking, but rather a reaction against the habit of intoxicated pedestrians to toss empty go-cups on the ground, and it caused an immediate flurry of concern among go-cup supporters. Ultimately, it resulted in so much disturbance in the drinking population (read: everyone) that the mayor's office felt the need to release a statement. The city, he assured concerned citizens, was not pursuing a universal ban on go-cups. Certain restrictions on go-cups do exist, however, in an attempt to reduce litter and noise. The consequences of this move are still unfolding. As it now stands, bar patrons in certain areas are being asked to bring their own go-cups instead of relying on those provided by bars.

DRINKING
IN NEW ORLEANS
TODAY

There is no other place on earth even remotely like New Orleans.
Don't even try to compare it to anywhere else.
—ANTHONY BOURDAIN

Today's visitor to New Orleans will find a cocktail environment that is both traditional and modern. Traditional because New Orleans only slowly incorporates trends into its cultural habits, and when one sticks, it really sticks. New Orleans has always been resolutely un-trendy. And modern because New Orleans bars are constantly inventing new and different drinks, and mixologists from around the world look to the city for inspiration.

The cocktail landscape in New Orleans includes excellent restaurant bars, hotel bars, and lounges, even terrific dive bars. Just take your pick. In the wonderfully modern establishments that have opened in recent years, bartenders embrace tradition as well as a twenty-first-century aesthetic. Many restaurants have bars that reflect this modern cocktail culture, enabling diners to order well-crafted cocktails at the table or in the bar. Increasingly, a restaurant's bar is a serious component of the overall dining experience.

According to Ti Martin of Commander's Palace, the landmark restaurant in the New Orleans Garden District, one of the often-unrecognized triggers of the resurgence of the cocktail in New Orleans was the 1999 publication of photographer Kerri W. McCaffety's lush coffee-table book, *Obituary Cocktail: The Great Saloons of New Orleans*. McCaffety's photographs are haunting evocations of another age, and are a beautiful ode to old local bars. Complete with recipes, the book celebrates the romance and mythology surrounding memories of cocktails in the city.

OBITUARY COCKTAIL

—— *Makes 1 drink* ——

This cocktail is a deathly spin on the martini.

2 ounces gin
¼ to ½ ounce (or less) French vermouth
An equal amount of absinthe

1. Place all ingredients in a cocktail shaker filled with ice. Stir until mixed.

2. Strain into a chilled cocktail glass. The drink will louche (turn a milky opalescence) in the manner of absinthe drinks. Serve ungarnished, and stark as death.

CORPSE REVIVER

—— *Makes 1 drink* ——

On those mornings when you wake up paying for the indulgences of the night before, a bit of reviving of the hungover corpse is in order.

1½ ounces brandy

¾ ounce applejack

¾ ounce sweet vermouth

Stir ingredients together in a cocktail shaker full of ice. Strain into a tall glass.

CORPSE REVIVER 2

—— *Makes 1 drink* ——

1 ounce gin

1 ounce triple sec

**1 ounce freshly squeezed lemon juice
    (or, if it is breakfast, orange juice)**

½ ounce absinthe

Stir ingredients together over ice in a shaker and strain into a tall glass.

The following is a sampling of the many restaurant and hotel bars and lounges in New Orleans that offer a well-crafted cocktail.

✦ COMMANDER'S PALACE ✦
1403 Washington Avenue

The Brennan family assumed the operation of Commander's Palace in 1974. From the start, they decreed that the restaurant would serve proper cocktails in the manner that New Orleanians and the Brennans had always enjoyed.

Ella Brennan, who managed the restaurant with her siblings, once traveled to Cuba and discovered that daiquiris there tasted better than those made in New Orleans. When she returned home, she tried to replicate the flavor of the Cuban daiquiris, using the same rum and even experimenting with the ice. Although she finally conceded defeat, her quest for the perfect daiquiri not only reflected her personal desire for excellence, but also, in a larger sense, signaled the importance of the cocktail to New Orleans.

Commander's Palace has evolved over the years, changing chefs and undergoing a huge renovation after Hurricane Katrina. It is now under the supervision of cousins Ti Adelaide Martin and Lally Brennan, the self-proclaimed Cocktail Chicks. As it has from the beginning, the restaurant reflects the traditions of the Brennan family, and also the traditions of New Orleans, by giving the same attention to making a drink as is given to preparing a dish.

When Ti Martin took control, she realized that bartenders at Commander's Palace needed just as much training as chefs, and she wanted her bar chefs trained by the best. She sent her crew to New York to learn under master mixologist Dale DeGroff at his Beverage Alcohol Resource (BAR). In doing so, she ensured that Brennan restaurants participated in the burgeoning craft cocktail movement. This course of professional instruction also ensured that Commander's Palace and other Brennan restaurants would become, in the words of executive bar chef Lu Brow, "spirited restaurants."

ELLA BRENNAN COCKTAIL
—— *Makes 1 drink* ——

½ ounce Sazerac rye whiskey

½ ounce Buffalo Trace bourbon

½ ounce cognac

½ ounce Calvados

1 bar teaspoon maraschino liqueur

2 dashes Angostura bitters

1 dash Peychaud's bitters

Lemon and orange twists, for garnish

Combine all drink ingredients in a mixing glass. Stir well and strain over ice into a cocktail coupe, or serve neat. Garnish with twists of lemon and orange.

❧ CURE ❧
4905 Freret Street

Cure is a cocktail lounge that serves food, allowing patrons to drink without having to eat lots of bar nuts to absorb the alcohol. Located in a repurposed fire station in uptown New Orleans, Cure was the brainchild of mixologist Neal Bodenheimer. When it opened in 2009, it was the first stand-alone, New York–style craft cocktail place in the city.

Cure's first bartenders, Kirk Estopinal and Maks Pazuniak, made a serious statement about their goals for the establishment by publishing a manifesto they called "Rogue Cocktails." The two stated forthrightly that they intended Cure to be an elegant place, and they called for equally elegant behavior and conversation to accompany their inventive drinks. Cure is no longer in need of such a broadside; it has the confidence of success. The original dress code, requiring long pants on gentlemen, has been abolished. But in a nod to the seriousness of the cocktail experience, bartenders still ask customers to remove their baseball caps.

Cure tries to be innovative and invites patrons to come along for the ride. Some of the drinks are an interesting amalgam of imagination and a rethinking of ingredients; other drinks are twists on traditional cocktail formulas. This is also a place with a point of view. Cure does not stock every brand of liquor, nor does it carry more pedestrian beers. One result of this avant-garde thinking is that Cure has been recognized nationally as one of the country's best bars, proving that New Orleans still has a place in cocktail history nationally, as well as keeping the flame alive and evolving at home.

THE END IS NIGH

—— Makes 1 drink ——

This recipe is from Cure, compliments of Neal Bodenheimer.

1½ ounces Rittenhouse bonded rye

1 ounce Bonal Gentiane-Quina aperitif wine

¼ ounce Varnelli Amaro Sibilla

2 dashes Angostura bitters

Orange peel for garnish

1. Place all drink ingredients in a cocktail shaker with ice. Stir 55 revolutions.

2. Strain into a chilled cocktail glass. Express an orange peel, which is used as garnish.

✦ FRENCH 75 ✦
THE BAR AT ARNAUD'S RESTAURANT
813 Bienville Street

Arnaud's Restaurant has figured in the culinary history of New Orleans since the establishment's founding in 1918. Like many restaurants of the early twentieth century, Arnaud's had a "Ladies' Entrance," through which women were escorted by men to be seated in the restaurant. There was also a men's-only entrance for the area reserved just for men—the Grill Bar.

In the 1940s, Count Arnaud's daughter, Germaine Wells, who was queen and maid of various Mardi Gras krewes, took over the restaurant's operations. An exhibit of her elaborate gowns, trains, and crowns, along with the scepters she carried through the years, can be seen at Arnaud's upon request. Germaine was known for her spunk and joie de vivre, which matched her father's. In taking on the ownership and management of Arnaud's, she made some changes, including opening up the Grill Room to women.

Today, this exquisite bar is called French 75. The name was adopted by the Casbarians, the current owners of Arnaud's, who renovated and reopened the Grill Room in 1979, adding a vintage varnished wood bar. In 2003 the bar was rechristened French 75 after the stiff drink, so named because its powerful effects bring to mind the formidable 75 mm field rifle used by the French in World War I.

The French 75 is tended by Chris Hannah. Hannah started his career in the food industry, but he found his home behind the bar. As a young man, he bartended in North Carolina, where his clientele averaged twenty to forty years older than him. These mature patrons tended to order classic cocktails, which he learned to make from a cocktail book. In the process, Hannah became immersed in the history and art of the cocktail. Now the French 75 provides classic cocktails such as the one below with the freshest ingredients. This is the feel of old New Orleans.

FRENCH 75

—— *Makes 1 drink* ——

2 ounces gin

½ ounce freshly squeezed lemon juice

1 teaspoon castor sugar

5 ounces champagne (Brut)

1. Place first three ingredients in a cocktail shaker with ice. Mix well to dissolve sugar.

2. Strain into a chilled champagne flute and top off with champagne.

❧ BELLOCQ ❧
THE BAR AT THE HOTEL MODERN
936 St. Charles Avenue

In the early twentieth century, professional photographer E. J. Bellocq privately took pictures of the inhabitants of Storyville, the famed red-light district of New Orleans. After Bellocq's death, those moving photographs were discovered, revealing a previously undocumented glimpse into life in Storyville. These images inspired Neal Bodenheimer, Kirk Estopinal, and Matthew Kohnke to create a hotel bar named Bellocq, which opened in 2011.

Bellocq house specialties are cobblers, the sweet, refreshing drinks popular in the nineteenth century. Cobblers were traditionally made with wines (especially fortified wines), sugar, fruit, and crushed ice. Bellocq also makes a cobbler variation with liqueurs, as well as more traditional cocktails.

KIRK ESTOPINAL'S
BONAL COBBLER

—— *Makes 1 drink* ——

Bonal Gentiane-Quina is a French aperitif infused with herbs that yield a complex flavor. The aperitif has a reputation of expanding the appetite, and starting a meal with this cobbler should make anyone hungry.

3 ounces Bonal Gentiane-Quina

1 level teaspoon superfine sugar

2 grapefruit peel swaths

Grapefruit slices and a strawberry or grapes for garnish

1. Place drink ingredients, including grapefruit peel, into a cocktail shaker. Shake briskly to mix ingredients and dissolve sugar.

2. Strain into a julep or rocks glass filled with crushed or pebbled ice.

3. Top drink with garnish composed of grapefruit slices and strawberry or grapes. Decorate to manifest your own vision of ornate beauty. Take your time to compose it. Two long straws plunged into the drink complete the garnish.

❧ CANE AND TABLE ❧
1113 Decatur Street

Cane and Table is another establishment from the owners of Cure and Bellocq. This one is a rum-and-sailor concept restaurant and bar located in the French Quarter near the Mississippi River. The bar menu celebrates the glory periods in the history of rum, especially evoking romantic notions of old Havana. Patrons can order rum punches, tiki drinks, and Prohibition-era drinks. Yet, while the bar is influenced by history, the touch is light. The restaurant's food is intentionally compatible with the bar's offerings.

IMPROVED BOMBO

—— Makes 1 drink ——

Recipe from Nick Detrich, bartender at Cane and Table.

1 ounce Plantation 5-year rum

1 ounce Smith and Cross navy-strength rum

¼ ounce Pierre Ferrand curaçao

1 teaspoon rich Demerara syrup

14 drops Bittermens tiki bitters

Ice

Freshly grated nutmeg

1. Build in a double old-fashioned glass by adding all ingredients except ice and nutmeg.

2. Add ice and stir 35–40 times. Garnish with nutmeg on top and serve.

☙ SOBOU ❧
THE BAR AT THE W HOTEL
310 Chartres Street

Inspired by the Brennan family's tradition, SoBou bills itself as a spirited restaurant. In the New York manner of naming neighborhoods, its name refers to "south of Bourbon Street." Although the bar is within the restaurant, patrons cannot escape the saloon feel of the place. Beer pulls adorn the tables and lighted bottles are everywhere.

SoBou lets you eat, or eat and drink—especially at the bar chef's table at the bar, which pairs drinks with food—or linger, as in a coffee shop. (There are outlets for laptops under each table.) A modern saloon or a reincarnation of the old New Orleans coffee shop—whatever you call it, it's fun.

GRAND DAME
—— Makes 1 drink ——

The following recipe was created by SoBou's lead bartender, Laura Bellucci, in honor of Ella Brennan, "who loved stingers." Laura says, "It tastes like a smoky, complex Junior Mint."

1½ ounces Famous Grouse scotch

½ ounce Fernet Branca Menta

½ ounce Tempus Fugit crème de menthe

2 drops vanilla extract

Mint sprig for garnish

Shake, strain, and serve up in a Nick & Nora glass. Garnish with a mint sprig.

❧ BAR TONIQUE ❧
820 North Rampart Street

Aside from serving excellent drinks, this bar has the feel of a delightful, unpretentious neighborhood hangout that has been around for a long time.

It's owned by the crew at Delachaise Restaurant in the Central Business District, which is also a casual place with high standards. Bar Tonique is located on the western border of the French Quarter, and it is friendly and welcoming, not at all like the tourist bars on Bourbon Street. The knowledgeable bartenders here use fresh ingredients. Although they're happy to reproduce the old standards, imagination is at play, with fine syrups, house-infused tonics, and house-made cherries making each drink exceptional and unique. Bar Tonique's goal is not purity of experience, but a happy customer. And temperance drinks are given the same care as alcoholic ones, so that even nondrinkers can enjoy themselves.

A great deal of thought went into this place, but the effect is subtle. It has the intimacy of a dive bar with the sophistication of a craft cocktail establishment. New Orleanians leave wanting to come back to this neighborhood bar, even if the French Quarter isn't their neighborhood. Maybe that's because Bar Tonique feels like a specifically New Orleans bar. It maintains the feel of the city, but also exudes modernity and attention to detail. That is an accomplishment.

❧ SWIZZLE STICK BAR ❦
IN THE LOEWS NEW ORLEANS HOTEL
300 Poydras Street

Established in 2003, this bar was arguably the first in New Orleans to focus on craft cocktails and was a part of the movement growing across the United States. Lu Brow, executive bar chef at the Commander's Palace family of restaurants and at the Swizzle Stick, makes a great cocktail and embodies that welcoming hospitality that is part of the bartending tradition. She knows the value of a traditional cocktail and has her own creations that feature freshly squeezed juices and her own bitters and syrups.

Brow is also known for nurturing young people in the industry. She is interested in New Orleans's cocktail history and in passing on that knowledge so that drinkers and bartenders can expand their cocktail experience. Brow was a member of the team that created SoBou.

❧ KINGFISH ❦
337 Chartres Street

This restaurant and bar, named for Huey Long's moniker, boasts the food of noted chef Nathan Richard, as well as the cocktail magic of Chris McMillian, *New Orleans* magazine's Bartender of the Year in 2012. McMillian's traditional hand with the cocktails is appropriate in a place that hearkens back to the Kingfish and his era.

☙ CAROUSEL BAR AND LOUNGE ❧
AT THE MONTELEONE HOTEL
214 Royal Street

The Carousel Bar and Lounge sports the only revolving bar still operating in New Orleans. A nod to the traditional amusement park carousel, it has a crown at the top and brightly hand-painted chairs. The revolution is relatively slow—about fifteen minutes to go all the way around—but fast enough to feel when seated at the bar. The carousel has been in the bar since 1949 and moves on steel rollers. The Carousel Bar was once part of a nightclub, the Swan Room, which operated in the 1950s and 1960s, and it was the site of musical performances by stars such as Liberace and Louis Prima.

The Carousel Bar is located in the Hotel Monteleone, founded by Antonio Monteleone. Monteleone was a Sicilian who came to New Orleans in the 1880s, the beginning of the great wave of Sicilian immigrants to the city. He started out as the owner of a shoemaking store on Royal Street and quickly realized that international commerce was transpiring in the city. With businessmen and travelers flocking to banks and French Quarter businesses, he decided to try his fortune in the hotel industry. Monteleone purchased the French Quarter Hotel in 1886. Soon the neighboring Commercial Hotel was for sale, and he purchased it as well, thus beginning the story of what has become the French Quarter landmark of today. In 1908, with the addition of three hundred rooms, the hotel's name was changed to the Hotel Monteleone.

Antonio's son, Frank, took over operation of the hotel upon his father's death, and he added another two hundred rooms in 1928. The

The Commercial Hotel, purchased and expanded by Antonio Monteleone. In 1908 it was renamed the Hotel Monteleone. (Collection of Chris McMillian)

Monteleone drink menu.
(Collection of Chris McMillian)

family maintained the hotel through the Great Depression and the ups and downs of the economy. In 1954, the original hotel was torn down as part of a major renovation and expansion. When Frank died in 1958, his son Bill Monteleone assumed the helm.

Over the years, the hotel has been like home to many visiting writers and celebrities. Ernest Hemingway and William Faulkner were habitués and frequent drinkers. Sherwood Anderson and Truman Capote also dropped in often, as did Eudora Welty and Tennessee Williams. In more recent times, Richard Ford and Winston Groom spent time there. The Friends of the Library Association named the Hotel Monteleone a literary landmark in 1999.

Many of the literary topers who stayed at the Monteleone had their favorite drinks. We can surmise that Hemingway drank absinthe there. In his short story "The Strange Country," which is actually a portion of the original manuscript of *Islands in the Stream*, the characters Roger and Helena stop in New Orleans on their drive west from Miami. They stay at the Monteleone and walk across "the old-fashioned marble lobby" on their way to "the air-conditioned bar." (The Monteleone was among the first establishments in New Orleans to have AC in the bar.) They decide to have absinthe, and even though the spirit is illegal (the story appears to take place early in the Spanish Civil War, around 1936), the waiter (wink wink) brings some of the real thing, in an ordinary Pernod bottle. Roger specifies that he wants Pontarlier absinthe, and when the waiter asks if he wants it frappé or drip, Roger asks for it dripped, but without sugar. Since absinthe is illegal, the bar lacks a traditional absinthe fountain, so Roger and Helena use saucers to drip the melting ice water into their glass.

When at the Monteleone, Hemingway likely would have had dripped absinthe with no sugar. But he would not have slowly ridden on his barstool around the Carousel bar, since it was not created until the late 1940s.

Hemingway brings the Monteleone into another story, too. In "Night before Battle," which takes place in a bar in Spain during the Spanish Civil War, two characters more or less reminisce about one evening at the Monteleone.

VIEUX CARRÉ
—— *Makes 1 drink* ——

The Vieux Carré is a signature drink of the Carousel Bar.

½ ounce Bénédictine liqueur

½ ounce rye

½ ounce cognac

½ ounce sweet vermouth

Peychaud's bitters

Angostura bitters

1. Mix together first four ingredients in an old-fashioned glass.

2. Add a dash of Peychaud's and another of Angostura.

3. Add ice and stir.

Ensuring that New Orleans remains at the center of the cocktail universe is Tales of the Cocktail, the world's premier cocktail festival. Founded by Ann Rogers Tuennerman in 2003, Tales is now operated by the New Orleans Culinary and Preservation Society, a nonprofit organization established in 2006.

The mission of Tales of the Cocktail is "to be recognized as the world's premier brand dedicated to the advancement of the craft cocktail through education, networking and promotion." And Tales promotes not only the craft cocktail, but also New Orleans. Every year, thousands of bartenders, bar owners, drinkers, and liquor industry representatives converge in July to drink, talk, and learn about new products and, of course, to enjoy the city. In the minds of many attendees, the keeper of the cocktail flame is New Orleans. Other places may be more cutting edge, more forward-thinking in trends and technology, but the heart and soul of the cocktail reside in New Orleans.

In the beginning, Tales was far from the elaborate and extensive event it is today. It began at the Carousel Bar in the Hotel Monteleone, when Tuennerman gathered a small group of well-known people from the cocktail scene across the United States, as well as local cocktail aficionados, to discuss cocktails. Tuennerman's goal was to bring attention to New Orleans and the emerging craft cocktail movement, as well as to the historic role the city played in establishing the cocktail as an American drink.

The rapid growth of Tales of the Cocktail has paralleled the increased interest in the craft cocktail movement throughout the United States. Purveyors of new spirits and liqueurs wait to announce their products at Tales, when so many bartenders and buyers are gathered together in one place. The ancillary events at Tales are just as appealing and enticing as the lectures, tastings, and spirited dinners. Awards given by Tales have become a matter of prestige and importance.

Although cocktail enthusiasts are welcome, Tales is aimed at those in the profession, with seminars, panels, and tastings designed to give bartenders and other industry pros new information and help them hone their skills. And through the annual event, Tales supports the Cocktail Apprentice Program. This program organizes about two hundred volunteers who work together to produce the huge volume of drinks necessary to supply the needs of the event. The apprentices work with top people in the industry, allowing them to learn from the best.

Another outreach effort of Tales is the Cocktail Apprentice Scholarship Fund, which makes funds available for education and research projects. For example, a scholarship supports study at the Crescent School in New Orleans. Winners report on their findings at Tales in subsequent years.

Tales allows people from all over the globe to come to New Orleans to drink and think and learn about cocktails. Despite competing events that have developed since the first Tales of the Cocktail, it remains the most important and prestigious, and it keeps New Orleans in the minds of bartenders worldwide throughout the year.

Fittingly, the Museum of the American Cocktail (MOTAC) was conceived over cocktails. It was the brainchild of master mixologist Dale DeGroff, who is credited with reviving the bar industry, resurrecting the cocktail from a morass of mixes, and educating bartenders on new standards of quality. According to its stated mission, the museum "celebrates and preserves a rich aspect of American culture" by educating the public and bartenders about the history of the cocktail.

The museum board chose New Orleans as the museum site because of the city's rich cocktail history. With an outstanding collection of artifacts, ephemera, and books, MOTAC is a treasure trove of material about the cocktail. MOTAC opened in 2005 on a floor above the Pharmacy Museum in the French Quarter—an apropos place to begin, the pharmacy being so intimately involved in the development of elements of the cocktail. Shortly after the museum opened, however, New Orleans was threatened by the imminent arrival of Hurricane Katrina. The city was evacuated and MOTAC's artifacts were boxed and safely stored.

Looking for a new home, MOTAC was offered refuge by the Brennan Cocktail Chicks. At the time, some members of the Brennan family were opening a Commander's Palace in a Las Vegas hotel, and they suggested that MOTAC exhibit the story of the cocktail on a wall at the restaurant, where diners could enjoy it. But the hotel was purchased and Commander's Palace was bought out, so MOTAC went into storage again.

Shortly thereafter, in July 2008, MOTAC opened a gallery within the Southern Food and Beverage Museum (SoFAB) in the Riverwalk Marketplace in New Orleans. It was open to exhibit visitors and for monthly programming for five years before becoming an official part of the SoFAB Institute in 2013. Its collection now can be seen in the new home of the Southern Food and Beverage Museum, at 1504 Oretha C. Haley Boulevard.

No matter where it went, MOTAC stayed connected to New Orleans. Why New Orleans? Not because the city was the place where the cocktail was invented. Not because New Orleans was the place where the word *cocktail* was coined. After all, the development of the cocktail was a social phenomenon and not something that can be credited to one person. MOTAC belonged in New Orleans because New Orleans was the place that nurtured the cocktail. The city was the keeper of the cocktail flame.

New Orleanians were early and enthusiastic supporters of the cocktail. In the first decades of the nineteenth century, New Orleans–based Antoine Peychaud developed a bitters formula still in use today, and became the first commercial producer of bitters—an essential element of traditional cocktails—in America. The Crusta (a precursor to the Sidecar), the Sazerac, and the Ramos Gin Fizz were all invented in New Orleans. In bars and at home, people learned to drink and savor the experience, took time to drink together companionably, and used the cocktail's intoxicating effects as both a social lubricant and a transcendent experience.

New Orleanians have always cared about the taste of their drinks. This is the city that saw the development of commercial ice, elegant saloons and hotels, and the great social customs of a culture that drinks.

With alcohol a part of its religious ritual, Creole Catholic New Orleans appreciated the importance of drink as a part of life. And with steamboats traveling up the Mississippi River from New Orleans to areas north, the word spread about the city and its cocktail practices.

As time marched on, New Orleans was recognized for its love and appreciation of spirits. Out-of-towners came to the city to partake, even though they often had not been properly initiated into the art and therefore did not understand the nuances of drinking.

It was also New Orleans that protected the cocktail during the dark days of Prohibition. And as the pace of life quickened in the twentieth century, New Orleans used the nightclub and lounge as new stages for enjoying drinks, proving that the city could evolve even as it clung to the principles of the past.

When the United States adopted powdered and bottled cocktail mixes and moved away from the cocktail to drink wine, New Orleans stayed the course. Even as convenience mixes infested some bars and trendy wine lists grew, well-crafted spirit drinks remained part of the culture, and New Orleans does not abandon culture. New Orleans certainly is tolerant of difference, but its paradox is that it is conservative and protective about its customs. Today, with the rise of the craft cocktail and the interest in older forms of drink, New Orleans continues to explore its drinking history, enjoy its strong present offerings, and anticipate the cocktail's future. So, cheers to New Orleans, a city that savors the cocktail, and one that sees the cocktail as a metaphor for savoring life.

À votre santé!

GLOSSARY

ABSINTHE. A spirit made from grape eau-de-vie. The distillate is flavored with various herbs, primarily anise, which are allowed to macerate. Absinthe traditionally contains grand wormwood, which was once banned by the Federal Drug Administration and the U.S. Department of Agriculture. Before its ban, it was a very high proof spirit that was often redistilled. Now it is sold at a lower proof.

ABSINTHE FOUNTAIN. Part of the paraphernalia used in the ritual of serving absinthe. The vessel contains water and ice, and has at least one spigot placed high enough for a stemmed glass to be placed under it. A glass containing absinthe is positioned under the spigot, and an absinthe spoon holding a sugar cube is suspended over the glass while the spigot flow is adjusted to allow chilled water to drip slowly over the cube. When enough water is in the glass, the spigot is turned off and the absinthe enjoyed.

ABSINTHE SPOON. A flat, trowel-shaped, pierced utensil placed over a glass containing absinthe. The utensil holds a sugar cube under the dripping water of the absinthe fountain as the piercings allow the water to pass through to the glass. The usually pointed end of the spoon is used to break up any sugar that has not dissolved.

AGING. The process of storing liquor in a barrel—usually oak, sometimes charred—so that the liquor absorbs both flavor and color from the wood of the barrel. The flavors absorbed depend on previous use of the barrel, age of the wood, and whether it is charred.

BITTERS. Tinctures of bitter herbs compounded by pharmacists for dosing patients as remedies for various ailments, from poor appetite to worms. Bitters were often placed into sugared spirits to make them palatable. When added to cocktails in small amounts, bitters add a complexity of flavor and depth. Peychaud's bitters are most closely associated with drinking in New Orleans.

BLENDED WHISKEY. Whiskey that is flavored, as well as colored neutral spirits; also, rectified whiskey.

BOURBON. An American whiskey required by law to be made from a mash of 51 to 79 percent corn. Other grains such as rye or wheat may form the rest of the mash. Bourbon may be aged two years or longer in charred oak barrels.

CASTOR SUGAR. A superfine sugar that dissolves easily and quickly, even in cold liquids. It is called castor sugar because its fine grains fit through the holes of a sugar shaker called a castor.

CHARRING. A method of aging, which colors and flavors the spirits, by placing the spirits in a wooden barrel that has been burned on the inside all around. The charcoal that is formed filters the spirits, and the spirits that are absorbed into the wood extract vanilla and caramel flavors and a reddish color from the barrel.

COBBLER. A slightly sweet drink made with either wine or spirits. It is garnished extravagantly with fruit and sometimes served alongside fruit.

COCKTAIL. At one time known as a bittered sling. A cocktail is a drink containing spirits, sugar, water, and bitters. There is controversy about whether a cocktail must contain ice, although the current practice is to at least chill the drink over ice. There is further controversy about the derivation of the word itself.

COCKTAIL SHAKER. A large metal glass into which the ingredients of a drink are placed, usually with ice. Another glass is placed over the shaker, forming a seal. The drink can be shaken as needed. The content is then strained into a glass, leaving solids and ice behind. An essential part of the bartender's tool kit.

COLLINS GLASS. A tall or long glass used to serve a Tom Collins and other drinks made with carbonated liquids such as soda water.

CONTINUOUS STILL. A mechanism that distills alcohol from a fermented product (distiller's beer or mash) on a continuous basis as long as it is being fed the product, using less fuel and creating a higher proof than a pot still.

CORDIAL. In the United States, a cordial is a liqueur, or a sweetened and flavored alcoholic drink. In Britain, a cordial is a fruit-flavored syrup often served diluted with water.

CRUSTA. The first mixed drink to include lemon zest and lemon juice as ingredients. It was served in a sugar-rimmed glass. Joseph Santini, a New Orleans bartender, is credited with its invention.

DISTILLATION. The process of vaporizing alcohol from a fermented product, using heat, and then condensing the vapors into a liquid, by cooling. The captured liquid may be heated and put through the distillation process again, or redistilled.

DISTILLER'S BEER. The distilling process requires a fermented product, and the thick fermented mash of grains and liquid that is poured into the still is called distiller's beer. Other vegetable matter can be added for additional flavor. Also called brewer's beer.

FIZZ. A spirited drink including a carbonated liquid such as soda water or sparkling wine.

FRAPPÉ. A drink served in a glass filled with cracked or chipped ice. Its novelty is that it is extremely cold. This type of drink became popular with the availability of ice.

GARNISH. The flourish of the spirited drink. It can be herbaceous, like a sprig of mint, to provide a whiff of refreshing and enhancing aroma with each sip. The garnish may instead be a fruit or vegetable, such as cucumber in a Pimm's cup or a lemon wheel on the rim of a glass. Some garnishes are purely decorative, like a cocktail pick or a paper umbrella.

GRENADINE. A red syrup, originally made with pomegranate, often used to color and flavor cocktails. Today, it is sometimes merely dyed simple syrup added for sweetness.

JACKING. A process of creating spirits without a still by freezing a fermented product and removing the water (as ice) as it freezes at a higher temperature than alcohol. By refreezing and refreezing, the proof of the spirits increases. This process can be dangerous as the amount of alcohol may be very high. A common American jacked product is applejack, made from fermented apples.

JULEP. Originally, a flavored syrup. It has now come to mean a spirited drink that uses a flavored syrup, a spirit, and ice, with or without sugar. The most common julep in contemporary times is the mint julep.

LIQUEUR. *See* Cordial.

LOUCHE. The cloudy appearance caused when oils that are alcohol soluble come in contact with water and become visible. This occurs in spirits in which herbs have been macerated, particularly anise-flavored beverages such as absinthe, Pernod, ouzo, and Herbsaint. The ability to create a swirling decorative louche is prized by absinthe drinkers. The louching process fascinated the demimonde of Europe. Such writers as Rimbaud and Oscar Wilde wrote about the hypnotic beauty of the louche.

MADEIRA. A fortified wine favored in early America and in colonial New Orleans.

MASH. The fermented product, both solids and liquids, that will be distilled to make spirits.

MINIMUM DRINKING AGE. Currently, 21 years of age throughout the United States, although for many years the minimum drinking age was 18 years old in Louisiana and some other states.

MUDDLE. To mash ingredients either in a glass or a cocktail shaker to express oils or juice or to dissolve sugar. The utensil used is called a muddler and was traditionally made of wood, but can be made of stainless steel or other materials.

NEAT. Bartender slang for a drink served in a chilled glass without ice.

NEUTRAL SPIRITS. Alcohol distilled without flavor. It can be flavored to make liqueurs or to mimic other liquors like bourbon or absinthe. It can also be mixed with other alcoholic beverages. This alcohol is generally distilled several times to remove other flavors, so it can be made from any number of distiller's beers. A neutral spirit is almost pure ethanol. In the United States, this means that it is distilled to over 190 proof. Also called rectified spirits.

OLD-FASHIONED GLASS. A squat, heavy glass that is solid enough to mix or muddle in.

OPEN CONTAINER LAW. This law can prohibit public drinking outside of a building, so that drinking outdoors at a park or picnic is prohibited, or it can allow carrying an open container in public, as in most of New Orleans, on Beale Street in Memphis, and in a few other limited locations in the United States.

POT STILL. A simple still that allows for the distillation of a fixed amount of mash or wort. The fermented product is heated, causing the alcohol in it to vaporize. The vaporized alcohol rises into a copper coil that is cooled, causing the alcohol to condense. The resulting liquid is then collected. To use the still again, the pot must be cleaned out and a new batch of mash added. Also known as an alembic still.

PROOF. The alcohol content of a spirit. The proof figure represents the alcohol content as a percentage of volume. You must halve the figure to determine the alcohol level. For example, "80 proof" means the spirit is 40 percent alcohol. The term "proof" really does derive from proving the merits of the alcohol.

The method of proof is to mix the alcohol with gunpowder and set it aflame. Under-proof spirits would be smoky and not burn, and over-proof spirits would create a huge flame. The term "100 percent proof" means that the spirit is 50 percent alcohol by volume and burns with a steady flame.

RECTIFIED WHISKEY. A blended, unaged, flavored, and colored spirited product made from neutral spirits that was often passed off as aged whiskey.

ROCKS. Bartender slang for ice. The phrase "on the rocks" or "over rocks" means that the drink is served with ice in the glass.

RUM. A spirit distilled from fermented sugarcane juice, molasses, or cane syrup.

RYE. A spirit distilled from a mash made from at least 51 percent rye grain. It is generally aged for at least two years.

SHAKE. To place ingredients in a cocktail shaker, usually with ice; cover the shaker with a glass to make a seal; and move back and forth vigorously to mix and chill the liquid.

SHRUB. A colonial-era drink made with vinegar syrup, liquor, and water. The sweetened, flavored vinegar used in the drink was also called a shrub. In England, the drink was popular in the seventeenth and eighteenth centuries, when it was made with fruit liqueur, citrus juice (which was replaced by sweetened vinegar) and/or citrus rinds, and spirits.

SIMPLE SYRUP. A solution made with either equal parts water and sugar, or one part water and two parts sugar. The mixture is heated to dissolve the sugar and maintain it in solution. Bartenders use this syrup to sweeten a drink because the sugar is dissolved completely, leaving no grit in the bottom of the glass. There is some dispute about the universal use of simple syrup as a sweetener, because it links the sweetening process with dilution.

SLING. A drink containing sugar, water, and spirits with a grated nutmeg finish. Also called a toddy.

SOUR. A type of cocktail with an acidic component as well as a sweet one.

SOUR MASH. The mash that results when leftover solids from a previous fermentation are used to start the fermentation process. This process usually results in a product that is consistent from batch to batch as the yeast is the same.

SPEAKEASY. A place where drinks were served during Prohibition (1920–1933), when it was illegal to produce and sell alcoholic beverages. Speakeasies operated in contravention of the law. They were frequented by many otherwise law-abiding citizens who simply wanted to drink alcohol in spite of its illegality. In an effort to protect themselves and their patrons, speakeasies often had steel or reinforced doors with a sliding slot. People entered after saying a password. Men and women who visited speakeasies drank alcohol out of coffee cups and resorted to other subterfuges to foil federal agents and other officials trying to enforce the law.

SPIRITS. A distilled alcoholic beverage.

STIR. The act of mixing ingredients with a spoon, in contrast to shaking them. When stirred with ice, the liquid is chilled, but not aerated.

STRAIGHT UP. Bar slang for a drink that is served chilled, but not over ice.

STRAIGHT WHISKEY. Whiskey that is aged and that has corn or rye as a predominant grain.

SWEET MASH. The mash that results when yeast is added to a grain mixture to start the fermentation process.

SWIZZLE STICK. A utensil used to stir a drink or hold a garnish. The original swizzle sticks were bits of a plant used to stir a type of rum punch called a swizzle. At one time they were made of glass, but today they are made primarily of plastic and are marked with the name of the bar for advertising purposes.

TODDY. A drink that can be served either hot or cold that contains spirits, water, and sugar, with a nutmeg finish. It was also known as a sling in the mid-nineteenth century.

UP. A spirited drink that is served in a chilled glass, but not over ice.

WHISKEY/WHISKY. This may be difference without a distinction. Tradition has it that when the name is spelled with an "e," the spirit is from the British colonies that broke from Britain (bourbon whiskey, Irish whiskey). When the name is spelled without an "e," the spirit is from Britain or its friendly colonies (Scotch whisky). There is inconsistency in spelling, however, that belies that explanation. George Dickel does not use the "e," and Early Times does.

WORM. The coiled copper tubing in a still into which the vaporized alcohol passes for cooling and condensation. The tubing is usually cooled during the distillation process by being passed through water.

WORMWOOD. The herb *Artemisia absinthium*. Also called grand wormwood, it is an essential ingredient in absinthe. It is also sometimes used to flavor vermouth.

WORT. The liquid that is left from the fermentation process when the solids are removed from the mash before distillation. Wort is commonly used in distilling scotch and other European spirits. By using only the liquid in the pot, the distiller reduces the chance of scorching, which is common with direct heat on the solids when the entire mash is heated. Scorching lends a burned taste to spirits.

NOTE ON SOURCES

In writing this book, we drew on a variety of sources. For the introduction, the following two books were especially helpful: David Wondrich, *Imbibe! From Absinthe Cocktail to Whiskey Smash: A Salute in Stories and Drinks to "Professor" Jerry Thomas, Pioneer of the American Bar* (New York: Perigee, 2007); Dale De-Groff, *The Craft of the Cocktail* (New York: Clarkson Potter, 2002).

For chapter 2, we relied on the following: Jon Kukla, *A Wilderness So Immense: The Louisiana Purchase and the Destiny of America* (New York: Knopf, 2003); Wondrich, *Imbibe!;* Leonard V. Huber, *New Orleans: A Pictorial History* (rpr. New Orleans: Pelican, 2014); Ted Haigh, *Vintage Spirits and Forgotten Cocktails: From the Alamagoozlum to the Zombie and Beyond* (Beverly, MA: Quarry Books, 2009); Ned Hémard, "Banana Republics and *Ojen* Cocktails," New Orleans Bar Association website, http://www.neworleansbar.org/uploads/files/OjenUpdate .3-2.pdf (accessed June 15, 2013).

For chapter 3: Haigh, *Vintage Spirits;* Janet Chrzan, *Alcohol: Social Drinking in Cultural Context* (New York: Routledge, 2013); Lafcadio Hearn, *La Cuisine Creole,* facsimile edition (New Orleans: Pelican, 1990).

For chapter 4: John Churchill Chase, *Frenchmen, Desire, Good Children... and Other Streets of New Orleans!* (rpr. New Orleans: Pelican, 2001), (Gallatin Street quote from this book); Al Rose, *Storyville, New Orleans* (University, AL: University of Alabama Press, 1974).

For chapter 5: Herbert Asbury, *The French Quarter: An Informal History of the New Orleans Underworld* (Garden City: Garden City Publishing Co., 1936);

William Head Coleman, *Historical Sketch Book and Guide to New Orleans and Environs* (New York: Astor House, 1885); George H. Devol, *Forty Years a Gambler on the Mississippi* (Cincinnati: Devol and Haines, 1887); Huber, *New Orleans: A Pictorial History.*

For chapter 6: Anthony J. Stanonis, *Creating the Big Easy: New Orleans and the Emergence of Modern Tourism, 1918–1945* (Athens: University of Georgia Press, 2006); Andrew Sinclair, *Prohibition: The Era of Excess* (Boston: Little Brown, 1962); Daniel Okrent, *Last Call: The Rise and Fall of Prohibition* (New York: Scribner, 2010); Joy Jackson, "Prohibition in New Orleans: The Unlikeliest Crusade," *Louisiana History* 19.3 (1978): 261–84.

For chapter 7: Haigh, *Vintage Spirits;* William Grimes, *Straight Up or On the Rocks: The Story of the American Cocktail* (New York: North Point Press, 2001); Wayne Curtis, *And a Bottle of Rum: A History of the New World in Ten Cocktails* (rpr. New York: Broadway, 2007).

For chapter 8: Jack D. L. Holmes, *New Orleans Drinks and How to Mix Them* (New Orleans: Hope Publications, 1973); Ti Adelaide Martin and Lally Brennan, *In the Land of Cocktails: Recipes and Adventures from the Cocktail Chicks* (New York: HarperCollins, 2007).

GENERAL INDEX

RECIPE INDEX